The Tao of Gestalt:
Poetry, Creativity and the Rediscovery of the Child

The Tao of Gestalt:
Poetry, Creativity and the Rediscovery of the Child

Brian O'Neill

Developed and Published by the Ravenwood Press a subsidiary of the Illawarra Gestalt Centre.
P.O. Box 141 Peregian Beach, Queensland AUSTRALIA.

Cover illustration, text design and art work: B O'Neill
Made and printed in Australia by University of Wollongong Printers

ISBN-9781479361809

For more information on Ravenwood Press
Email: boneill@uow.edu.au
Website: www.illawarragestalt.org
 Or write to

Brian O'Neill
Illawarra Gestalt Centre
P.O. Box 141 Peregian Beach, Queensland
Australia

Contents

Dedication

This book is dedicated to my sons
Benjamin O'Neill and Samuel O'Neill
(Sam and Ben)
who have consistently shown me the
Way (Tao) since they were born.

Foreword

My first thought on reading earlier drafts of this still resonating book was that "Fools rush in where angels fear to tread".

Gestalt psychotherapy is a discipline in which even the first two words of the sentence you are now reading - including the capital "g"- is enough to evoke/provoke polemics. Note how I partly solved this by having to capitalise the "g" as the first word in a new sentence, and thus sidestepped the ire of colleagues who insist on "gestalt therapy" (Bloom, Spagnuolo-Lobb, Staemmler). So for an established Gestalt practitioner to publish such an apparently unorthodox perspective as Brian O'Neill does here can clearly be regarded as courageous. Well acquainted as he is with the sometimes reverential and even defensively proprietorial attitudes towards the primary texts of "gestalt therapy", his courage could also be seen as a touch of foolishness...though more in the spirit of Saint Francis, perhaps, than of any court jester.

And yet, and yet...I know Brian O'Neill to be a versatile and creative Gestalt practitioner with individuals, couples and groups; a sought-after manager in mental health and family support settings; I know him to be successful in co-founding, co-running and co-leading with his wife Jenny the longest ongoing and much respected Gestalt training centre in Australia. In gestalt therapy circles internationally he is acknowledged to be theoretically daring while simultaneously well grounded in such a primary text as *Gestalt Therapy – Excitement and Growth in the Human Personality* (Perls, Hefferline & Goodman, 1951), generally known as *PHG*.

I personally know him to be a man of *faith* in many of the meanings of that characteristic: spiritually as a student of Buddhism, Taoism and the mystical Christianity of Emmanuel Swedenborg (Brian is an ordained minister of the Swedenborgian *New Church* in Australia); and also a man of *faith* in the existential sense of Kierkegaard and Sartre and Goodman. To all of the above can be added the particular sense of *faith* peculiar to physicists in general and quantum physicists in particular – as you will read, Brian's first academic subject was physics.

This was followed by English literature and psychology. Psychology then became Gestalt psychotherapy, and a long and thorough reading of *PHG*, not only as a student and then practitioner, but also as a trainer, institute leader and author.

So, to the extent that Brian O'Neill may or not be an angel, he is clearly no fool...nor is he exactly "rushing" in: the contents and themes of this book have been taken in, processed, synthesised and integrated over almost a lifetime of learning, practice and experience.

These themes include the fundamental theoretical framework of Gestalt psychotherapy as well as its consequences both personally and professionally. These he places firmly in the context of Hinduism, Buddhism and Taoism – as well as the thinking of Martin Buber, the philosophy and poetry of William Wordsworth, aspects of Christian mysticism, and, of course, the life and times of Brian himself as he holds and expresses the unity and unifying power of these influences on him and then offers his integration of them to us as his gift. Brian's often daring and always creative syntheses are presented with the confidence of one who has thought through his theoretical approaches, put them into practice, and is now able and willing to share his conclusions with us.

Emmanuel Swedenborg – Swedish mystic and spiritual writer – and long a major influence on Brian's life, practice and thinking has claimed that "nothing unconnected ever happens" (Swedenborg 1768). This book is a good example. Here, Brian has allowed these connections in his life to emerge as an integrated whole, calmly containing its various and apparently disparate parts while at the same time giving them meaning, both in themselves and in relation to each other. To risk a paraphrase of Wordsworth: all of these dynamic themes and their connections "roll" through Brian, their intrinsic poetry expressed in his quiet prose.

Central to this book is a reading of *PHG* that is as idiosyncratic as it is informed. As the second of the two core gestalt therapy texts - the first is *Ego, Hunger and*

Aggression (Perls F. & L., 1946) – *PHG* has become the object of everything from reverence, to criticism to contemporary revision. Brian O'Neill has chosen a specifically situated perspective – that of Taoism – to provide a contextual focus for his reading. In other words, he starts by connecting to far back in time as well as far away in space and, thus, connecting also to the core text itself: "Gestalt is the original, undistorted approach to life" (PHG, 1951, pg 218). He continues by adding links from his other chosen sources to create a rich matrix of interconnected themes.

Any attempt on my part to introduce and/or explicate these themes in this Foreword would be to rob the reader of the experience of meeting them as the author intends – in effect, rob the reader of meeting Brian O'Neill in who he was, is and has become and all that he represents of his journey to here-and-now.

A foretaste of the richness and creative connections intrinsic to this volume can be found in the topics and people referenced in the list of contents and bibliography. I urge the readers to whet their appetite already there, and to then move on to the *smörgåsbord* of people and themes within the covers of this both evocative and provocative book.

A good *smörgåsbord* is an invitation to taste and savour what is on offer before selecting what to chew and swallow. I invite you, dear reader, to taste, savour, select and enjoy yourself, as I have done.

Seán Gaffney Ph.D
Dublin, 2012/2013.

Preface

By the time I turned sixteen I had lived on three continents (Europe, North America and the Australia). Then for over a quarter of a century I lived in Australia and knew no other country, including my native Ireland. For those who know Australia it is a unique land, mostly desert yet with significant beautiful coastal strips along East and West coasts, where almost all the population lives. It also has unique animals and flora, from the kangaroo, echidna and platypus, to the Gymea Lilly and the beautiful Illawarra flame tree.

So when I left as an adult to attend the first Association for Advancement of Gestalt Therapy (AAGT) conference in New Orleans you can well believe I was amazed at the differences even between such similar Westernised cultures as the USA and Australia. Equally so people were quite amazed meeting an Australian (though of Irish origin) and so began a phase of my life and my family's life where we regularly visited the USA (and people from there came here to Australia) which then spread to Europe with conferences and workshops there.

At the end of this travelling I realised two things - almost so glaringly obvious I am a little shy to say them - everywhere I went was different and this was fun. And everywhere I went was remarkably similar and this I find interests me just as much.

So it is with this book. I have spend more than thirty years in the land of Gestalt therapy while I have visited many other different countries, some of whom needed time travel to read about and venture into their frame of reference, such as the ancient Taoist writings. I have traveled to the land of poetry and literature, to the creative arts and my great enjoyment of movies and music, and to an ever present experience of love and wisdom manifesting as spirit in the religious writings of the many different faiths and spiritual practices. These lands offer me the creative turn which happens as we allow the 'adult' nature (seen as neurotic) which is so busy with "habitual deliberateness, factuality, non-commitment and excessive responsibility" (PHG, 1951, pg 305) to be quiescent and open to a wider space of being.

I am not promoting to 'attach' such themes as spirituality, poetry, of the recollection of the child as 'new' bits for Gestalt therapy. I have already found them in the seminal text and it is the comparision with other 'lands' and the similarities and differences I have expereinced that I have written about and offer for your consideration. My own travels to the USA and Europe have given me a greater appreciation of Australia, both for its difference and similarity. Metaphorically I hope this book will offer the same for those who 'live' in Gestalt therapy as we venture to other 'lands'. As I write about these other 'lands' I have taken the liberty (or duty in a book about creativity) to include Chinese painting and quotes from Taoist sources, as well as my poetry.

For those of you who bought my book *Our Search for Meaning: Essays in Gestalt Therapy and Spirituality*, I have included an essay from that book which I thought essential for this book - *Being Present to the Emergent Creation of the Field: Wordsworth, Buber and Gestalt Therapy*. In that book it was simply another essay in a collection, yet as I wrote this book I realised it belongs here - it fits and is at home.

Finally allow me to thank and acknowledge my dear friend, colleague, brother and lighthouse, Seán Gaffney. While my sons have shown me the Way he has consistently along with Jenny endeavoured to keep me on it.

Brian O'Neill
Peregian Beach, January 2013

"Returning is how Tao moves

Yielding is how Tao functions

All things in the world are born from Fullness

Fullness is born from Emptiness."

Tao Te Ching

Introduction

"Our approach in this book is 'unitary' in a sense that we try in a detailed way to consider every problem as occurring in a social-animal-physical field."

(Perls, Hefferline and Goodman 1951, pg 218)

My approach in this book is unitary to subjects that have previously been written about separately - the interconnecting threads in Gestalt therapy between creativity, poetry, and the rediscovery of childhood. These threads are further elaborated by the spiritual perspective of the Tao or Way, also found in the text of Perls, Hefferline and Goodman (1951). The reason I would write on these subjects makes sense when you understand my background.

My early intent was to be a nuclear physicist and I studied this at university for two years. However I found that, unlike the exciting ideas presented by our teacher at high school, my university lecturers focused on mathematics almost to excluding anything else. This was not for me and I changed to study psychology which had taken my eye. Indeed I did a double major with another topic I was interested in, English Literature. I won't mention the implicit irony of this, being Irish, but then I just have.

I came close to becoming an English literature major (and teacher) for a time instead of a psychologist. I was fascinated with poetry and specifically that of Wordsworth. His poetry connected with the depth of my being. I found I could read and understand him as easily as breathing or eating breakfast. I felt a connection and union with him and his subject matter, transported to his world.

"And I have felt
A presence that disturbs me with the joy
Of elevated thoughts; a sense sublime
Of something far more deeply interfused,
Whose dwelling is the light of setting suns,
And the round ocean and the living air,
And the blue sky, and in the mind of man
A motion and a spirit, that impels
All thinking things, all objects of all thought,
And rolls through all things."

(Wordsworth, W.
"Lines composed a few miles
above Tintern Abbey")

This was a difficult choice to make between psychology and literature. One of the defining events which shaped my life (and therefore choice) was the appearance of Dr.

Don Diespecker in the third year of study in psychology. Don was fresh from training in San Diego with noted Gestalt therapists Erving and Miriam Polster. His counseling classes included gestalt therapy workshops and I began attending and training in Psychodrama and Encounter groups. Adding to exciting experiential therapies, Don was passionate about the newly emerging Transpersonal Psychology. This included the work of people such as Charles Tart and Richard Ornstein who studied Altered States of Consciousness and wrote about the 'psychologies' of the East such as Buddhism and the Sufi.

Wordsworth and his poetry faded in comparison as I experienced the glorious latter end of the cultural revolution of the 1960s with Hippies, counter culture and such. Yet this was transforming into the decade of the seventies and the flashy dance of the Disco era. I think I believed I was equally "flash".

Whatever seeds were sown then in my love of poetry, many of which faded and disappeared, there remained an imprint of remains which flowed deeper in my being. These seeds occasionally surfaced more and more, at times of distress or of ease and lightness. I can feel these remains or seeds now bearing a fruit. My past is bringing together within me a coalescence of these seemingly different influences of poetry, therapy and spirituality into a unified field of my experience, understanding and knowledge.

I hope this process I am experiencing and describing is as useful for you in reading the book as it is for me in the writing.

33

Pi/Holding Together (Union)

The Image
On the earth is water:
The image of Holding Together.
Thus the kings of antiquity
Bestowed the different states as fiefs
And cultivated friendly relations
With the feudal lords.

"Water fills up the empty places on the earth and holds tight to it. Water flows to unite with water, because all parts of it are subject to the same laws. So too should human society hold together through a community if interests that allows each individual to feel themselves a member of a whole."

I-Ching, pg 37
Wilhelm, 1950

Prologue

There was much discussion about the genesis of the 'self' in a recent lively, even heated, and scholarly discussion on the email list for the New York Institute of Gestalt Therapy (NYIGT). Our conversations went to which came first, organism or self and is the self a property of the field or of the individual. True to form the discussion went from this 'either/or' position to one of 'both/and' and Bud Feder (also true to form) came in with a pithy quote:

> *"I have heard talk of the beginning and the end, but I do not talk of the beginning or the end.*
>
> *There has never been more inception than there is now"*
>
> Walt Whitman

The Paradox of the Self

A re-evaluation of the idea of self is needed in reading and practicing gestalt therapy as it is in spiritual teachings such as Taoism and Buddhism. It must be remembered the teachings of Lao Tzu, Confucius and Buddha took place within particular languages, cultures and eras.

When current Buddhist literature talks of an "ego-personality" it seems out of place, as these are terms more in keeping with 19th and 20th century psychology. The ancient mystical teaching refers simply to the "self" – and this term "self "is a translation from another language.

At the very least we must be careful when hearing terms such as self and ego, and realise that they may have a different meaning than intended. This is equally true in the current use of these terms by various psychological theorists. There is as much divergence in the modern psychological use of these terms as there is between Buddhist texts and current English translations.

Even with issues of language, culture and era considered - the paradox of self still exists. The Buddha's teaching is that we suffer because we invest our identity in a state of being which involves birth, death, sickness and decay. This is called 'self' and it is this which leads to all sorrow and troubles.

Paradoxically there is another state of being which we can experience. A state of being which is not attached to the six conditions of human existence – and this is Buddha-nature. While Buddha-nature is different from this "ego-personality", it also very closely resembles it – and herein lies the paradox.

This paradox is perhaps most evident in the Tibetan Book of the Dead where we read:

"Recognising the voidness of thine
own intellect to be Buddha-hood,
And knowing it at the same time to be
thine own consciousness,
Thou shalt abide in the state of the
Divine Mind of the Buddha".

The Tibetan Book of the Dead
W.Y.Evans-Wentz. 1927

The self is void, an illusion. At the same
time it is us, our "self," who experiences
this. Putting these together we experience
the Holy, in this case the Divine Mind of the
Buddha.

Carl Jung (1927) when writing in the
psychological commentary to the Tibetan
Book of the Dead argues the state of mind
required to accept and understand such
paradoxical statements in not readily
available in Western society. Western
society, he states, is medieval and
unenlightened in attempts at understanding

theology and philosophy at this level. This often leads to a denial of paradox and the need for an "either/or" classification of self and the soul. You either lose your self or find your self... you can't have both!

However he states writings such as those of Mahayana Buddhism and the Tibetan Book of the Dead speak of a deep humanity and insight into the human psyche and readily embrace such paradoxes with a magnificently affirmative "both/and!" In losing ourselves we find ourselves. There is a gentle Buddhist story which explains this.

The Mother and the Sick Child

There was a mother who had a sick child and she took the child to see a doctor. The doctor saw the child needed medicine which he gave to the mother. However the child needed time to digest the medicine so the mother was instructed not to breast feed the child until this had happened and the child was ready for milk. The mother anointed her breasts with a bitter ointment so the child would not smell the milk and keep away. After the medicine had been digested, the mother cleansed her breasts and let the child suckle. The mother did this because she loved the child.

In the same way we are told, Buddha, to remove misunderstanding and attachment to ego-personality (or self) denies the existence of self; and when misunderstanding and attachments are done away with, he explains the reality of the true mind that is Buddha nature. This maps out a process of self experience. At first we must somehow discover or comes to terms with the voidness of our "self". This re-evaluation is a new awareness which paradoxically leads to awareness at the same time that this is our consciousness.

It is in this paradoxical state, in which we are both empty and full, that leads us to dwell in the Divine Mind of the Buddha. In some ways the paradox of the self we have been speaking of is not solely something that belongs "out there" in the writing of these sacred texts. It is paradox which comes from the blurred vision we bring in our attempts to enter an understanding and experience of these teachings. Mystical and religious texts abound with this common theme - an understanding of self connects with that which is beyond the self. This leads to the experience of self being grounded in the Holy:

"Therefore the sage puts his self last
yet his self is first
He treats his self as extraneous,
yet his self is preserved
Because he is without selfishness
his self can fully develop

Tao Te Ching
Lao Tzu, page 32

As we shall read about later in the book the same paradox of the nature of self is found in the early writing of gestalt therapy, as much as in the current email list discussions. An early gestalt therapist, Wilson van Dusen, who brought Fritz Perls to the West Coast USA, in writing on spirituality and existence stated:

"That we are in the midst of conflicting theories of existence is really a delight. We must find out what is true for ourselves to find the way in all this richness. Our existence thankfully is far from simple."

Van Dusen, 2001, page 130

In the next chapter we now enter in to a midst of confirming theories and travel between these various lands of poetry, creativity and rediscovery of the child - all embraced within a Tao of Gestalt - a delight.

45

"That which lets now the dark, now the light appear is Tao.

It gives life to all things, but does not share the anxieties of the holy sage. Its glorious power, its great field of action, are of all things the most sublime.

It possesses everything in complete abundance: this is its great field of action. It renews everything daily: this is its glorious power.

As that which completes the primal images, it is called the Creative.

In that it serves to infuse an organic coherence into the changes, it is called the work"

Lao Tzu

The Tao of Gestalt Therapy

"In ideal circumstances the self does not have much personality. It is the sage of Tao that is 'like water,' assuming the form of the receptacle."

(Perls, Hefferline and Goodman
1951, pg 427)

If a poet, physicist or Buddhist read the text of Perls, Hefferline and Goodman (1951) - *Gestalt Therapy: Excitement and Growth in the Human Personality,* we might wonder what would stand out and how would they connect with the writing, if at all. The word used in the title of this book "Tao" is also in the seminal text of Gestalt therapy, and many readers of Perls, Hefferline and Goodman (PHG) might not notice this. Ruth Wolfert (2000) did notice and she wrote one of the few essays I have read which talks about Taoism and Gestalt therapy (also Lynne Williams in the Gestalt Review 2006).

Wolfert states -

> "*Gestalt therapy is a holistic therapy with a greater spiritual foundation than is utilized by most Gestalt therapists. It is based, in part, on teachings from Buddhism and Taoism.*"
>
> (Wolfert, 2000)

During a detailed read of *Gestalt Therapy: Excitement and Growth in the Human Personality* years ago I noted words such as "Tao", "soul" "faith" "spirit" and even "angel" are to be found, however the angel use I am sure is colloquial. These terms are in the "second" book, written mainly by Paul Goodman. The use of these terms is understandable knowing Goodman's background and writing. These terms may carry little meaning until they are understood within the context of the theory in which they are found. As I read these instances, particularly those where the terms "Tao" and "soul" occur, it seems obvious Goodman was both a spiritual and potentially religious person. Other authors such as Sylvia Crocker note this and describe Goodman in this way (Crocker, 1999). The "soul" for example is used in several occasions as an alternative version of 'self' as in the following:

> "*Of the chief classes of contact-functions, feelings are most often considered the underlying self or 'soul'; this is because feelings are always spontaneous and middle; one can neither will nor be compelled to feel something*"
>
> (Perls, Hefferline and Goodman, pgs 376-377)

In describing the *method* of psychology, Perls, Hefferline and Goodman (PHG) make a curious statement and one which demands more attention. They state that this method is to proceed from the objects of experience to the acts to the powers –

"...from the nature of the visible to the actuality of sight to the power of seeing as part of the organic soul".

(Perls, Hefferline and Goodman, pg 391)

Clearly this statement resonates with other mystical and spiritual writing, especially the work of Martin Buber. What is conveyed has an ineffable quality and speaks to the shift in levels of awareness described by many who write, as Buber does, of spiritual experiences. It describes a 'movement' from the visible reality (which in writings on the Tao is an 'appearance') to the 'actual' of our seeing nature, to finally describe a sight which links nature and the spiritual in being able to see with the 'organic soul'.

"The wind blows over the lake
and stirs the surface of the water.
Thus visible effects of the invisible
manifest themselves.'

I-Ching, pg 235

Wilhelm, 1950

Crocker states the Greek idea of soul deeply influenced Goodman's thought and thus Gestalt therapy (Crocker 2005 pg 163). Such terms have dissolved into the theory of Gestalt therapy and now later emerge as unanswered riddles which have become a tension for some in Gestalt therapy.

Perls, Hefferline and Goodman also discriminate between the terms 'soul' and 'self'. They state the "*system of conservative inherited adjustments is the physiology*" (pg. 400) - what the ancients called the 'soul' and psychology is the science of the soul. They go on to make a distinction that the subject of psychology is the special set of physiological adjustments for what is NOT physiological "namely contact at the boundary in the organism/environment field" (pg 400).

Dare I say that in this statement it could be argued they are bringing together the spiritual influences of the past definitions of "soul" by the ancients with the contemporary field theory of physics and psychotherapy?

Whatever position the soul is allocated within *Gestalt Therapy: Excitement and Growth in the Human Personality* the Tao is mentioned plainly as that which Goodman holds obviously as valuable.

The Tao is used by Goodman to describe being in the world in a way which confirms the unitary approach of the book and offers the salvation to insecurity and suffering. Further the description of the Tao is closely connected with the valued state of the 'middle mode' of functioning and especially the return to the experience and value of being a child.

The book states that when things are deranged the concept of self regulation by the functions of the soul is met with anxiety and rejected as nihilism. They go on to offer a solution to such anxiety and say -

> "*But we reiterate that the suggestion is a spectacularly conservative one, for it is nothing but the old advice of the Tao, 'stand out of the way'.*"

> (Perls, Hefferline and Goodman,
> pg 247)

Suffering

The application and advocacy Goodman offers of the Taoist 'Way' becomes clear both when the term "Tao" is used and as an undercurrent in how it is suggested we, the reader, can deal with a variety of life's ups and downs, blessings and joys. In discussing the meaning of suffering within this newly forming "gestalt" perspective we read how there arises from our conflicts - whether within social collaboration or the struggle of the poet - a means to lessen the pain and reduce our suffering. This is an age old question that has been asked and with answers sought throughout the ages of mankind.

The meaning of suffering is one of the foundational questions of religions and spiritual practices alongside our search for meaning in life, and this includes how to deal with such suffering. It is of key importance in the work of William James, specifically in his text *The Varieties of Religious Experience* (James, 1902). Once again the writer(s) state they resort to the more ancient wisdom of the Tao -

"How in fact do they finally lessen the pain?

By finally 'standing out of the way,' to quote the great formula of the Tao. They disengage themselves from how it 'ought' to turn out. And into the 'fertile void' thus formed, the solution comes flooding."

(Perls, Hefferline and Goodman,

pg 378-379)

Security

The counterpoint to suffering can maybe considered as security - secure from suffering and harm. This is similar to the story of Buddha where he defines the Noble and Ignoble Paths as two contrasting ways to deal with suffering. The first way, which he calls the *wrong* way, is to ignore the awareness of sickness, old age and death and seek the opposite in the pleasures of life.

In the alternate way to be with such suffering, which he calls the *right* way, the person is to recognise the transitory nature of this ego state and physical reality, and *search for meaning that transcends it.*

This story of the Buddha parallels what Perls, Hefferline and Goodman describe as our need to seek security. Similar to the Buddha and his description of the Ignoble Path, the writer(s) state that holding to a sense of security in life is a weakness because we are always waiting for its disproof to happen. The Buddha offers the Noble Path as the solution, while Perls, Hefferline and Goodman offer that meaning in life's suffering is found in the present moment through cultivating a sense of "readiness." This readiness is closely connected to their description of artists and children being in a "middle mode" of neither overtly directive not passive - what the writer(s) state is akin to what theologians call "faith".

By having faith in our sense of readiness and acceptance of our excitement, a sense of sense of adequacy and power grows -

"A sense of adequacy and power grows as the particular problem is met and generates its own structure and new possibilities are found in it, and things surprisingly fall into place." (ibid, pg 415).

As Lao Tzu states in the writing of the Tao Te Ching:

> *"There are those who want to control*
> *the world by action.*
> *But I see they cannot succeed.*
> *The world is a sacred vessel*
> *It should be not interfered with*
> *To interfere is to spoilt it*
> *To grasp it is to lose it."*
>
>
>
> *Tao Te Ching:*
> *The Way of Nature and its Powers*
> Lao Tzu
>
>

These descriptions of Taoist teachings and the writing of what Perls, Hefferline and Goodman describe as a way of being in the world which counters the anxious and controlling mode of many adults and organisations in the modern world. There is a richness in connecting Buddha, Lao Tzu and a modern psychotherapy where each have similar language as striving to describe states of being which provide a sense of hope, joy and excitement.

In particular it is Goodman's emphasis on the recovery of childhood (as he rescues it from the psychoanalytical restrictions of Freud) that the emergent figure of *Gestalt Therapy: Excitement and Growth in the Human Personality* shines.

"A child leaves off capriciously, but while he is engaged he gives himself. The adult, partly because he is so preoccupied with being so responsible for himself, gives himself less earnestly. Again, it is only the

gifted person who retains this ability of childhood..." (ibid pg 304)

And it is perhaps surprising (or not to some) that these existential statements by PHG on how to live with suffering aided by the 'middle mode' of the child and poet are found in the writings of current Christian mysticism -

> *"...the rediscovery of childhood and consequently the perceptive appreciation of the secret surprise of customary objects is a very rare and precious kind of experience, enjoyed almost exclusively these days by unspoiled children."*
>
> (William McNamara, 1979, pgs 57-58)

While enabling your body and
soul to embrace oneness -
are you able to do it without
needing to be secluded?

When focusing your vital power
and becoming soft and yielding -
are you able to be like an
infant?

Lao Tzu

The Rediscovery of Childhood

"The childish feelings are important not as a past that must be undone but as some of the most beautiful powers of adult life that must be recovered: spontaneity, imagination, directness of awareness and manipulation."

(Perls, Hefferline and Goodman, 1951, pg 297)

A significant part of the second book of *Gestalt Therapy: Excitement and Growth in the Human Personality* returns time and again to several interrelated themes which centre on a shift in our state of being which is existential and for many experienced as spiritual. If we use the saying, that to *know* something is knowledge, to *understand* it is intelligence and to *live* it is wisdom (Swedenborg, 1992/1768) then so much of what is written in the text offers knowledge and understanding. How to offer wisdom though, a 'lived' experience of what is being written about? As we read in their (PHG) critique of verbalisations and detachment from experienced reality, this knowledge and understanding is useless unless lived, it is empty - just so many words.

The hope for this 'lived wisdom' they are writing about comes in an unexpected way through the agency of the child, the poet and the artist. The greatest critique offered by this text (PHG) may be the authors offer their paradoxical schemata for developmental psychology which involves "the recollection of childhood" when Freudian Analysis was such a potent psychological force. We are asked to consider that traditional notions of maturing and developing are at best half the picture and it may be that our idea of what is "mature" as opposed to what is "infantile" may have been generated from a linear developmental paradigm which sees growth as being from childhood up to adulthood and stops there.

Perls, Hefferline and Goodman offer a path to a progressive integration of the conflicted and polarised self that clients or patients present with in therapy in describing the 'lived wisdom' (or state of being) which enables people to find harmony and wholeness in a world of suffering and challenges. As an alternative to an analysis of the "problems" brought to therapy for healing by analysis or behavioral modifications, a richer poetic alternative is offered in the way of 'being in the world of the artist and child'. This is not a unique proposal, and as Goodman alludes to, this is found in the wisdom of the ancients and the Tao. It is also something others in the fields of arts and literature, music and spirituality describe which they are at home with. The same if true for sports people, those engaged with the elements such as surfers and those in sailing. In describing the way of being in the world by artists and children Perls, Hefferline and Goodman define an awareness that is a:

"...kind of middle mode, neither active nor passive, but accepting the conditions, attending to the job, and growing towards the solution. And just so with children: it is their bright sensation and free apparently aimless play that allows the energy to flow spontaneously and come to such charming inventions" (ibid, pgs 245-246).

Linked to this 'middle mode' state the Tao stands for and describes a state of 'being in the world' which confirms the unitary approach of the book and offers the salvation to insecurity and suffering. The description of the Tao is also closely connected with the valued state of the middle mode of functioning and especially the return to the experiences and value of being a child.

It is perhaps worth expressing this process of the middle mode again-

- *accepting conditions*
- *attending to the job*
- *growing towards the solution.*

They go on to state that in both the artist and the child the aspects which allow this to happen are

- *sensory-motor integration*
- *acceptance of the impulse*
- *attentive content with the new environment*

Children, Sages and Clowns

This conceptualisation of such creative processes and experiences is perhaps less "new" today than it was at the time that

Gestalt Therapy: Excitement and Growth in the Human Personality was written. More recently a Christian mystic, William McNamara, who has read and connects with Fritz Perls, offers in his writing the same experiences and understanding of this creative state. He describes this not solely from within a psychotherapy frame, where the role is for healing, but from a spiritual frame where the focus is healing of body, mind and soul, and with greater emphasis on the 'soul' than Perls, Hefferline and Goodman.

> *"In this age of immense sophistication, vast achievement, and jaded sensibilities, the rediscovery of childhood and consequently the perceptive appreciation of the secret surprise of customary objects is a very rare and precious kind of experience, enjoyed almost exclusively these days by unspoiled children, uncanonized*

saints, undistinguished sages and unemployed clowns

If we follow the lead of the child, the sage and the clown we may learn to discover and celebrate the sacred within the profane and respond to divine disclosures in both the squalor and splendour of the world. They are, each in his own unique way, at home with things, seeing the shining insides and detecting all the mysterious connections among creatures.

They overcome polarities and reconcile opposites. With keen insight and cosmic inscape they can feel the tremors and vibrations of the whole earth. This kinship with all is what makes them superbly compassionate".

(William McNamara, 1979, pgs 57-58)

Describing middle mode and the recollection of the child is a challenge for the psychotherapy trainer and/or supervisor in Gestalt therapy. How might we offer training in *'middle mode'*? This challenge to 'train' students in the experiential and existential aspects of these writings of the *'middle mode'* and the creative space of children and artists requires a trainer worth their salt who is familiar with and can provide training spaces for others to experience this process and not just understand it.

This requires a pedagogy (or andragogy) providing an integration of knowledge, understanding and living of these states of being which the book describes. Otherwise the training is like airplane pilots sitting in a class learning aeronautics yet never flying a plane.

If we consider the principles of these philosophical statements outlined above, it requires experiences of the student being able to be -

- accepting of conditions
- attending to the job
- growing towards the solution.
- sensory-motor integration
- acceptance of the impulse
- attentive to the newly emerging environment

The challenge to train people in these experiences is the reason so much of the training in Gestalt therapy has been in the form of demonstration workshops and personal therapy. An additional element which McNamara, the Polsters (with the Contact Episode and point/counterpoint) and Fritz Perls added to this 'middle mode' (which students find helpful and profoundly simple), is the method of how to work with our experience of polarities and to "reconcile opposites", as McNamara describes.

At first this was Perls' stereotypical 'two chair work' yet this can reduce the gestalt approach to a "paint by numbers" training which loses the essence we are striving for.

By 1975 Perls, in the more spiritually minded text *gestalt is* (purposely with a small "g"), described working with polarities as being the basic philosophy of Gestalt therapy, while in another text that is more clinical he describes it as Phenomenological Behaviorism (Perls, 1970, in Fagan and Shepherd).

> "*The basic philosophy of gestalt therapy is that of nature - differentiation and integration. Differentiation by itself leads to polarities. As dualities these polarities will easily fight and paralyse each other. By integrating opposite traits we make the person whole again*".
>
> (Perls, in Stevens 1974, pg 7)

As a trainer I find the use of Perls work with polarities and 'Two Chairs' at first seems profoundly simple and offers the trainee to move between technique and the skills and competencies of working with polarities. This is a titration between being a practiced behaviour and authentic behaviour, a stepped approach to learning. However it is in the use of the words "we" and "make" in this quote from Perls the shift from the middle mode of Perls, Hefferline and Goodman is seen to subtly slip into a "we" *treating* others solely as "patients" and "making" them whole again.

To do therapy as described by Perls would return us as therapists to the more directive and controlling frame of the adult and in essence lose the middle mode of the child and artist.

So caution is needed to not confuse the support and titration of 'paint by numbers' exercises which students learn from, for our willingness to move from a directive (and secure) state to one of 'being present to the emergent creation of the field.'

Unfortunately many people even today equate the gestalt approach with this showmanship of the dramatic techniques and demonstrations by Perls, where the gestalt approach is seen as a cathartic and confronting psychotherapy approach.

This is not to argue against being directive or at various points taking more responsibility for the therapy session than the client when (for example) they are suicidal. Clearly this warrants a degree of clinical and trainer/supervisor skill and discernment. Freud made an interesting comment when defining therapeutic alliance where there is the balance of helping the part of the person that is disordered or even psychotic while not doing for the person what they can do for themselves.

William Anthony in describing a Recovery Model for mental illness states:

"Recovery is described as a deeply personal, unique process of changing one's attitudes, values, feelings, goals, skills and/or roles. It is a way of living a satisfying, hopeful and contributing life even with the limitations caused by illness. Recovery involves the development of new meaning and purpose in one's life as one grows beyond the catastrophic effects of mental illness"

(Anthony, 1993 pg 3)

He states the basic assumptions of a Recovery Focused Mental Health System are that professionals do not hold the key to recovery - the consumers do; and a common denominator in recovery is the presence of people who believe in and stand by the person in need of recovery; that recovery is not related to theories of cause;

recovery can occur even though symptoms reoccur; recovery changes the frequency and duration of symptoms; and recovery does not feel like a linear process. There is a balance being described here by both Freud and Anthony that allows for both the more directive work of Perls imbedded in his statement above and found in his two chair methodology, and the more fluid Taoist philosophy of the writing of Perls, Hefferine and Goodman.

For it is with the practice of the "Middle Mode" and the "Rediscovery of the Child" that gestalt therapy comes into its own and stands apart from so many therapies which are directive and seek to "heal" the person in the way a surgeon would do. In line with William Anthony, we do not hold a key to a person's recovery from mental illness, we can provide a presence and believe in and stand by the client, and as our experience of the middle mode shows, healing and recovery are not linear and oft times paradoxical.

If we are to stay with these seeming opposites of *directive* Two Chair work and the *Middle Mode* of the Recollection of the Child, then something connective is needed. The work of the Erving and Miriam Polster provides a solution which bridges and connects. It is through their focus on 'being present' and working with the client as they experience both the point and counterpoint of their existential dilemma. Their theory and teaching of two seeming opposites (point/counterpoint) which develop into a third position as a synthesis of the two, provides a more fertile ground to integrate opposites. It is neither modern nor novel, nor do they claim this. In philosophy, the process of dialogue and the theory of the dialectic can be traced from Plato and Aristotle through to Kant and Hegel (Hamyln, 1987) and in psychotherapy it is found in the work of psychoanalysts such as Jung (1927) and Assagioli (1973). The Platonic idea of synthesis and antithesis which becomes a third new creation or "synthesis" stepping us beyond polarities into a new birth is found in many different forms of psychotherapy.

What is novel in the work of the Polsters is that the profoundly simple map of the "Contact Episode" can be taught and applied using the principle of point/counterpoint to explain a "theory of practice". In their work they are offering a map to guide the beginning therapist and the client on their journey through the complexity of the therapeutic session and move beyond the struggle with polarities to a third state of synthesis.

Perls, Hefferline and Goodman offer that 'spontaneity, imagination, directness of awareness and manipulation of the situation' can come into play for both therapist and client in the therapy session.

The therapist through their training and supervision and the client in their struggle with suffering, are hopefully both becoming more than a child or an adult - they can experience the synthesis of both child and adult as being *'wise children'*.

Developing through Un-developing

Wordsworth gives enough indication in his poetry to suppose that he was a mystic and well aware of spiritual states and stages of development. His poetry is rich with natural mysticism of the type well known to mystics such as Martin Buber and also in tune with the idea of the *Recollection of the Child* in Perls, Hefferline and Goodman. This "recollection of the child' is resplendent throughout much of his poetry. His poem *Intimations of Immortality from Recollections of Early Childhood,* is a model of human development where childhood through to adulthood is one of spiritual devolution or un-development.

"Our birth is but a sleep and a forgetting;
The Soul that rises with us, our life's Star,
Hath had elsewhere it's setting,
And cometh from afar:
Not in entire forgetfulness,
And not in utter nakedness,
But trailing clouds of glory do we come
From God, who is our home:
Heaven lies about us in our infancy!
Shades of the prison house begin to close
Upon the growing Boy
But he beholds the light, and whence it
flows,
He sees it in his joy;
The Youth, who daily further from the east
Must travel, still is Nature's Priest
And by the vision splendid
Is on his way attended;
At length the Man perceives it die away
And fade into the light of common day.

Intimations of Immortality From
Recollections of Early Childhood,
William Wordsworth

This is a marked contrast to the traditional models of psychological development. Here people are developing in body and mind, at a cost to the soul (or spirit) which becomes overshadowed in this development of the physical and psychological. Wordsworth describes the beginning of this developmental journey to be *"trailing clouds of glory"* as the infant state of being forms. This is our greatest connection to God, our home - what Swedenborg calls *"remains"*. As the psyche or ego forms and develops we become less aware of these states of being, less able or wanting to breathe this rarefied air or walk in such sunlight. We become grounded in this world of appearances slowly and insidiously until our memories of this state of being in which Love and Wisdom abound, fade *"into the light of common day"*.

Traditional developmental psychology outlined the stages of Infancy, Childhood, Adolescence, Adulthood and Old Age as the markers of our growth to maturity. In comparison to this adult-centric perspective Wordsworth outlines the journey between infancy and adulthood in this poem as follows:

Infancy

Our birth is but a sleep and a forgetting;
The Soul that rises with us, our life's Star,
Hath had elsewhere it's setting,
And cometh from afar:
Not in entire forgetfulness,
And not in utter nakedness,
But trailing clouds of glory do we come
From God, who is our home:
Heaven lies about us in our infancy!

Childhood

Shades of the prison house begin to close
Upon the growing Boy
But he beholds the light, and whence it flows,
He sees it in his joy;

Adolescence

The Youth, who daily further from the east
Must travel, still is Nature's Priest
And by the vision splendid
Is on his way attended;

Adulthood

At length the Man perceives it die away
And fade into the light of common day.

It would indeed be sad if that was the end of our development as a person. Yet it is at this point as adults when we reach our mature state as physical and psychological beings, that the internal call to return home to these earlier states of childhood appears, and we hear the call for the 'Recollection of Childhood'.

As with the story of the Buddha, everyone is called in to consider their life one way or another and move from our ego-bound life of the Ignoble Quest and discover the Noble

Quest in which we experience moving beyond our ego. It may be through illness or death, through a gentle change in life, through marriage or child rearing, or in the pursuit of what you love doing best. Whatever way it happens the call goes out. Some hear straight away and are ready and respond. Most struggle with the call and move back and forward between the world of appearances and the spiritual reality that surrounds us. Some fight the call and the stronger the call and the stronger the fight the greater the illness that results. Many get lost in the appearance of job success, of financial security or any of the treasures which we attach to so easily. Others turn the call into a battle with their demons or the demons of other people and miss the 'clouds of glory'. And many try to sedate the call with drugs and alcohol and food - feeding the physical until it weights down the soul with its gravity of biological processes. This call to change is like the caterpillar which will metamorphose into a butterfly or a raindrop which will eventually join an ocean. We are continually growing and developing, and feel and sense these changes from the limited perspective of our "self".

As Perls Hefferleine and Goodman state it is the organism, not the self that grows - the self is the Agent of Growth. This is the ground of our being, in which we are figures which emerge and form and return to close the Gestalt. Not to disappear though. For it is as we discover this seeming voidness of our consciousness, that we also realise that we are conscious at the same time and in holding these two polarities a paradoxical change take place.

This was described earlier quoting Carl Jung as he introduces the Tibetan Book of the Dead when he quotes the paradoxical change that is experienced as the person surrenders to the creative void beyond their "ego state" -

"Recognising the voidness of thine own

intellect to be Buddha-hood,
And knowing it at the same time to be
thine own consciousness,
Thou shalt abide in the state of the Divine
Mind of the Buddha".

The Tibetan Book of the Dead
(W.Y.Evans-Wentz, 1950)

In discovering this voidness behind our appearance of ego existence to be Buddha-hood and still our own consciousness, we dwell in the divine mind of the Buddha. We experience states of awareness where the illusion of the world of appearances begins to fade. We begin to recollect, sense and feel our child nature once again, this time with adult minds.

Whatever fuels this *Metanoia* in the end may not matter. We change. We turn. We re-turn. And as we return in our developmental cycle which has at first seen the diminution of the soul state and the growth of the mind, another cycle happens.

The soul grows big again and the mind takes its proper place.

So our soul life appears to grow. In reality this is all of us that grows, body mind and soul, as we are not separate souls and minds and bodies. We are a unity like a caterpillar which may eventually metamorphose into a butterfly. Like a raindrop which will eventually join an ocean. We are continually growing and developing, and feel and notice these changes from the limited perspective of our "self". As Perls Hefferleine and Goodman state it is the organism, not the self that grows - the self is the Agent of Growth.

What a different picture we would see if we could view ourselves through the eyes of our partner or our family or God.

It is this spiritual development, which begin at this turning point, the mystics, religious and spirituality writers are describing. This connection with the "more than self" now becomes crucial. The experience of a wider field of influence, a greater force, a power that as Wordsworth describes -

"...rolls through all things."

This ground of our being, in which we are but figures which emerge and form and return to close the gestalt. Not to disappear though. For it is as we discover this seeming voidness of our consciousness, that we also realise that we are conscious and in holding these two polarities does a paradoxical change take place.

Peter Pan and Captain Hook

To do this of course we must reconnect with the child in us which began with this experience. In modern dreams of the cinema this is so well created in the movie *'Hook - The Movie'* with Robyn Williams and Dustin Hoffman.

The original Peter Pan story is about not wanting to let go of these 'clouds of glory' and refusing to grow old - a case of stultified development. Yet the beauty of *Hook the Movie* is that Peter Pan does grow old. He becomes a boring busy accountant adult. He forgets how to be bigger and wilder. It is only through the shadow figure of Hook coming and stealing what is precious, his children, does he set out to re-find that which is important to him. Similar to Jung's description of the Shadow in our consciousness, the Shadow figure of Hook works to bring back to reality the adult lost in the illusions of the world of appearances. To save the day, Peter must remember how to be a child again. Remember how to fly and fight the shadow. To win back that which is most precious - Love. To restore order in the chaos of the adult psyche that has grown to feel so important and central to running the universe. The global dream maker of movies portrays a much more advanced psycho-spiritual model of development than the seemingly learned traditional texts. Perhaps Wordsworth and Spielberg have more in common with Swedenborg and Jung than they do with Erikson and Piaget.

Child, Adult and Wise Child.

This description of a development process which begins as seeming devolution of the 'soul' with which the infant is graced, happens so an ego-state may develop of a "separate" personality. As this personality develops and matures, the state of spiritual connection to the 'All' from which the infant is born, begins to fade. Finally it is *as if* this spiritual nature has vanished and the person has become what is seen by many as the height of development - they have become an Adult.

Yet the world of the Adult is such that they realise this is not after all the end of the affair. Processes are at work which returns the adult to connect with the state they were born out off, and the Adult moves to become a Wise Child. This model of development it is found in some form or other in the mystical teachings of all the major religions of the world across time.

"The concept of an 'ego-personality' is something that has been imagined by a discriminating mind which first grasped it then became attached to it, but which must abandon it. On the contrary Buddha nature is something indescribable that must first be discovered. In one sense, it resembles an ego-personality but it is not the ego in the sense of 'I am' or 'mine'"

Bukkyo Dendo Kyokai page 150

This true nature of the person, like the Kingdom of Heaven in the Gospels, is described by parables and metaphors in Buddhist teaching. It is the moon hidden beneath the clouds, a precious stone hidden in the dust and dirt of personal interests, the sacred medicinal herb hidden under the wild growths of the Himalayas.

Spiritual development requires the person to melt the ore and remove the impure substances of worldly passions and egotism to recover this pure Buddha nature.

Taoism and the I Ching

The Tao Te Ching and the I Ching describe these developmental processes with poetry which is succinct, paradoxical and rich:

"Returning is how Tao moves
Yielding is how Tao functions
All things in the world are born from
Fullness
Fullness is born
from Emptiness."

It is in the return to this *Innocence of Wu Wang* the true nature of the spirit is realised and the person is devoted to the divine spirit within. From here as a Wise Child the person reaches an "unsullied" innocence without personal attachment, our Fullness is born from our experience of this 'emptiness" of nonattachment. Both polarities are required and one cannot exist without the other. As we read in Perls Hefferleine and Goodman the childish feelings are important not because they are a past that must be undone but more so because they are the most beautiful powers of adulthood that must be recovered -

"... spontaneity, imagination, directness of awareness and manipulation. What is required, as Schactnel has said, is to recover the child's way of experiencing the world; it is to free not the factual biography but the 'primary process of thought' "

(Perls, Hefferline and Goodman,

1951, pg 297)

Judaism

The work of Martin Buber is a continuation of this tradition of development by the recovery of childhood and reflects this in Judaism. Buber mirrors Fritz Kunkel (1984) describing the "*We-Experience*" of the young child, when he writes how our initial state in the womb of the mother is '*I-Thou*'. This is before we recognise a sense of "I". In speaking of the life of the child in the womb he echoes Wordsworth ("trailing clouds of glory") when he refers to the Jewish saying, that it is in the mother's womb the person know the universe, and in birth forgets it.

"Every child that is coming into being rests, like all life that is coming into being, in the womb of the great mother, the undivided primal world that precedes form. From her, too, we are separated and enter personal life, slipping free only in the dark hours to be close to her again, night by night this happens to the healthy man. But this

separation does not occur suddenly and disastrously like the separation from the bodily mother; time is granted to the child to exchange a spiritual connection with the world that he gradually knows. He has stepped out of the glowing darkness of chaos into the cold light of creation".

(I and Thou, Martin Buber page 25)

The development of 'I-It' is made possible by this separation of the 'I' from the rest of the world. In this separation process, in the same vein as Wordsworth, the person's development happens by a step forward into this world of "self and objects" and now relates to the world as the objects of its perception. Lacking direct access to primitive man to discuss the development of these primary words of *I-Thou* and *I-It*, Buber turns to the child and sees in the infant the cosmic connection and the birth out of the universal.

99

"The world has a beginning

The mother acts as the beginning of the world

By finding the mother, know her children,

By knowing her children, follow the mother"

Lao Tzu

Wordsworth and Buber describe common pathways for this paradoxical process of ego development and parallel "un-development". This is a growing divide between the forming ego state (PHG's adult) and the state of being "universal" which the child is born out off. Visually this is conceptualized in the following diagrams:

Source of Creation

unborn person

○

"In the mother's womb
the person knows the universe"

Martin Buber

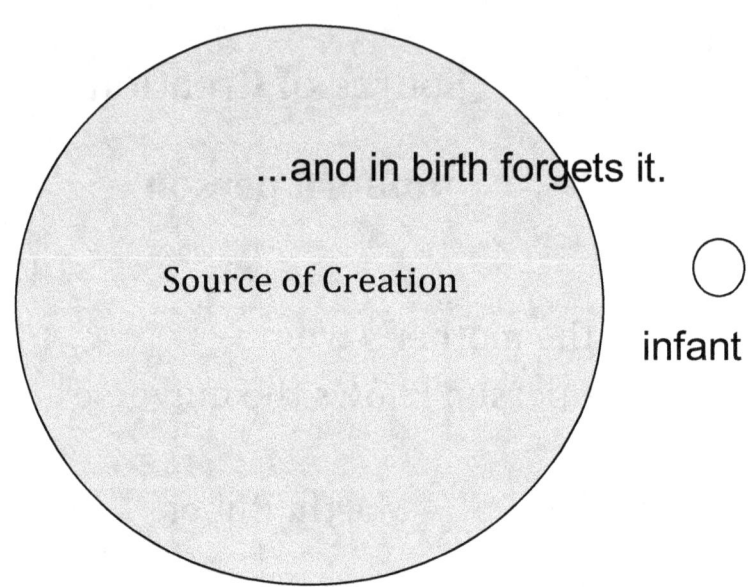

...and in birth forgets it.

Source of Creation

infant

Our birth is but a sleep and a forgetting;
The Soul that rises with us, our life's Star,
Hath had elsewhere it's setting,
And cometh from afar:
Not in entire forgetfulness,
And not in utter nakedness,
But trailing clouds of glory do we come
From God, who is our home:
Heaven lies about us in our infancy

Infancy

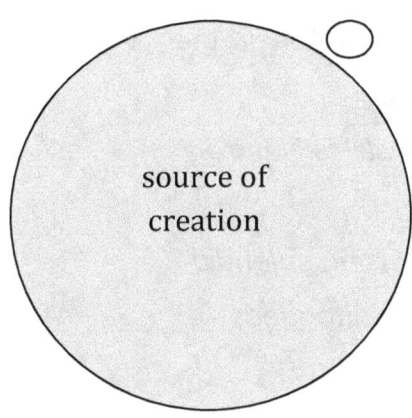

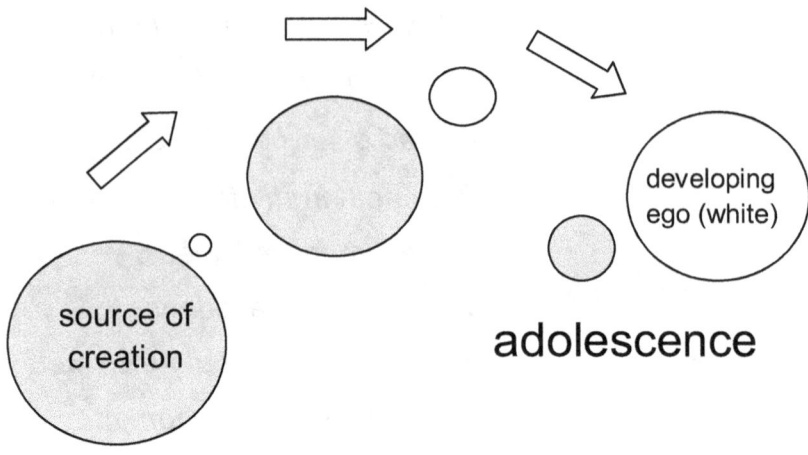

The Youth, who daily further
from the east
Must travel, still is Nature's
Priest
And by the vision splendid
Is on his way attended;

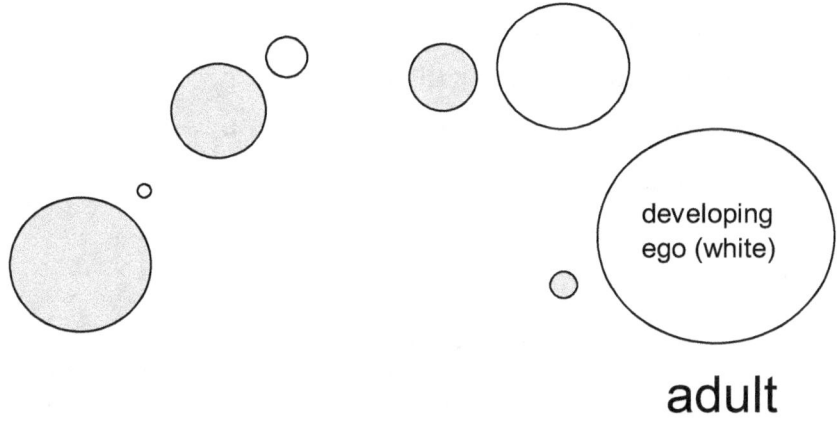

developing
ego (white)

adult

At length the Man
perceives it die away
And fade into the light of
common day

This state of the Adult might continue for a long time, even until death, yet there occurs for everyone a major life event that precipitates a change in this field and leads to what for many is a life change or "metanoia".

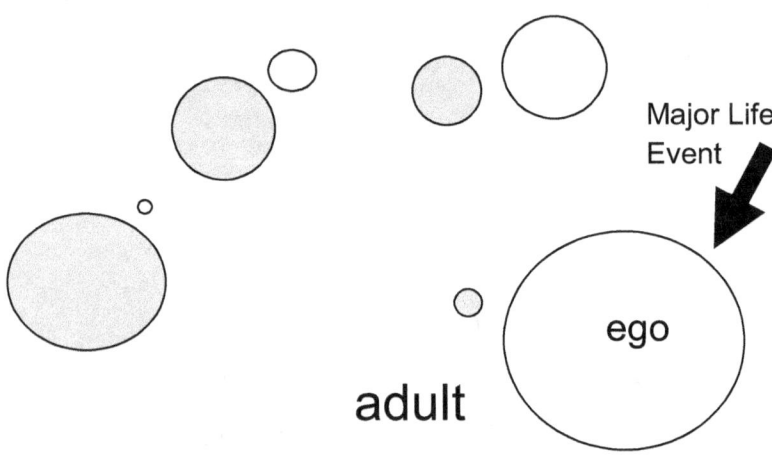

"Metanoia" in a theological sense is described as changing our mind, repenting for our ways, and turning around. This turning around in this diagram has a wider and more figurative meaning, as we are "turning around" to return to the source of our being, often through what has commonly been called a mid-life crisis.

Arthur Deikman (1982) gives an example of where a group of psychotherapists were meeting, originally for peer supervision, but soon the group began to deal with what they termed their mid-life crisis.

"The mid-life crisis with which the psychotherapists grappled probably reflects the fact that at midlife one's own death becomes less theoretical and more probable. Goals of money, security, fame, sex, or power might formerly have given purpose to life. With experience, the limited nature of such satisfaction becomes increasingly evident.... As life progresses the search for meaning becomes increasingly urgent."

The Observing Self:
Mysticism and Psychotherapy
Arthur Deikman, page 7.

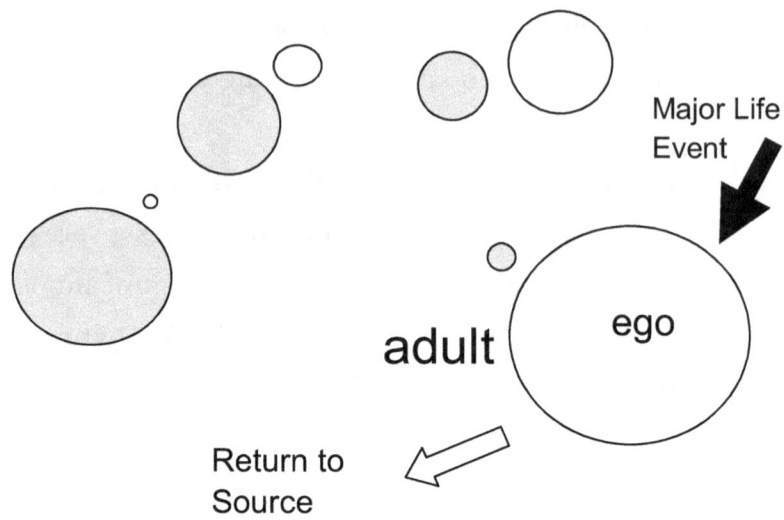

Our noisy years seem moments in the being
Of the eternal Silence: truths that wake,
        To perish never:
Which neither listlessness, nor mad endeavour,
        Nor Man nor Boy,
Nor all that is at enmity with joy,
Can utterly abolish or destroy!
    Hence in a season of calm weather
        Though inland far we be,
Our souls have sight of that immortal sea
        Which brought us hither,
    Can in a moment travel thither,
And see the children sport upon the shore,
And hear the mighty waters rolling evermore.

In the chapter on the "*Maturing, and Recollection of Childhood*", Perls, Hefferline and Goodman (mostly Goodman in the main), critique the Freudian formulae of

adult = mature

and

child = infantile

They describe how the recovered memory work in therapy by the adult involves the faculties of being habitually deliberate, a need for factuality, non-commitment, and and excessive responsibility, which add to the neurosis. However the child, like the poet, brings to these situations the powers of spontaneity, imagination, earnestness, and direct expression of feelings which are healthy. Hence their formulae are instead:

adult = neurotic

and

child = healthy

They do not wish to separate or polarize these two states of development and being. What they suggest is in harmony with the development and un-development of Wordsworth and Buber, a "Recollection of Childhood" - a reclaiming of these states of being closer to the universal harmony from which we are born. As they state:

> "For our thought is that the content of the recovered scene is rather unimportant, but that the childish feeling and attitude that lived that scene are of the utmost importance. *The childish feelings are important not as a past that must be undone but as some of the most beautiful powers of adult life that must be recovered*" (italics in text)
>
> (Perls, Hefferline and Goodman, 1951, pg 297)

This completion of the cycle and the rediscovery and recollection of childhood may be described visually as follow

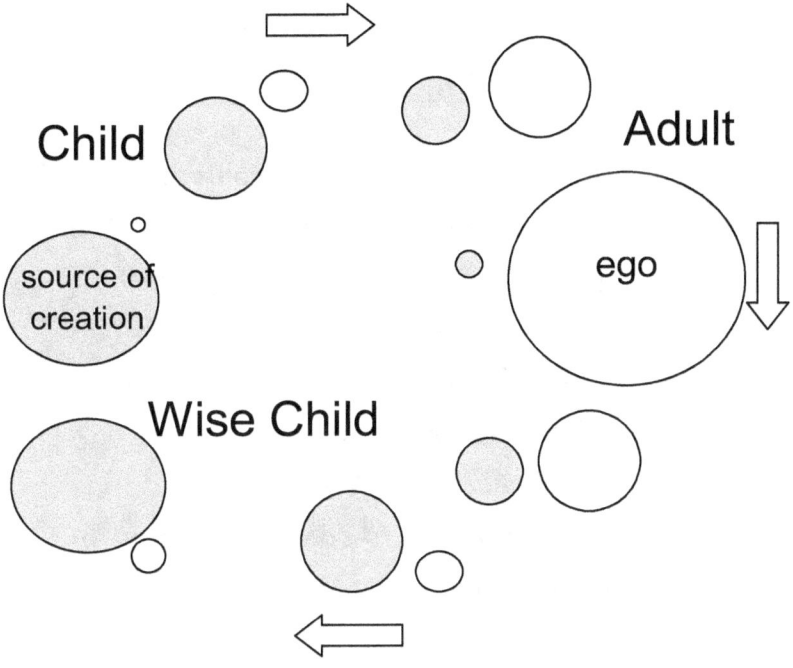

In the next chapter we consider the shift that happens for us as we progress in our development to "recover the child" as adults. This plays an important role not only in reducing the mental disorders and stress that are experienced in the life of so many people but in returning us to a source of great creativity and life, in which paradoxically and poetically "actively surrender" and come into a greater harmony with the Tao.

"There is a great need in contemporary society to rediscover the 'holy'. The holy does not refer to any specific religious belief, but rather to an opening-out to that which is beyond us. It is the repression of the holy, the out-of-touchness with the holy, that has helped create such a dangerous state of affairs in the world today."

Between Person and Person: *Towards a Dialogical Psychotherapy Richard Hycner, p.24*

BLUE SKY

The blue sky of childhood
restores my soul.
Sheltered in sunlight,
touched by sea breezes
moving in the leaves.
Is choice so valued
in the Harmony of all things
the abuse of Innocence
is a consequence?
The soft eyes
show the pain
of knowing Good and evil
which in the storm of the Holocaust,
is seemingly forever.
It is this Age which says that God is dead.
The morning's comfort
is found in the gentle silence
as sunlight warms the wooden floor.
Somehow I am blessed
by the eternity of the mundane -
a gentle breath of innocence
pervading all things.

Ch'ien / The Creative

"Great indeed is the generating power of the
Creative;
All beings owe their beginning to it.
This power permeates all heaven"

Confucius

Creativity and Gestalt Therapy

"When I feel well and in good humour, or when I am taking a drive or walking after a good meal, or in a night when I cannot sleep, thoughts crowd into my mind as easily as you could wish. Where do they come from? I do not know and I have nothing to do with it.

Those which please me I keep in my head and hum them; at least others have told me that I do so. Once I have my theme, another melody comes linking itself with the first one in accordance with the needs of the composition as a whole; the counterpoint, the parts for each instrument and all the melodic fragments at last produce the complete work.

Then my soul is on fire with inspiration. The work grows; I keep expanding it conceiving more and more clearly until I have the entire composition finished in my head although it may be long. Then my mind seizes it, as a glance of my eye would a beautiful picture or a handsome youth. It does not come to me successively, with various parts worked out in detail, as they will later on, but it is in its entirety that my imagination lets me hear it."

Wolfgang Amadeus Mozart

This process experienced by Mozart is a study in the key elements of the creative process and significantly similar to the description of the "middle mode" by Perls, Hefferline and Goodman. It is almost identical to that described by an early gestalt therapist, Wilson Van who worked alongside Fritz Perls and Carl Rogers (amongst others) and brought Perls to the West Coast to live with him. He writes

"I often write from beyond myself, surprised at the rich flow of thought and turn of phrase. For days before I begin I sense inner concerns formulating themselves. Suddenly I know I ready to write because sentences and ideas whirl

around in my head. I'm accustomed to it now. That's how it is. I'd be quite unable to take full credit for it. Influx. It is given. Life is given. Sensation given. Its all given."

Wilson Van Dusen

(personal communication, 1984)

Creativity has been part of the Gestalt therapy lexicon since the seminal text and several books have been written about it within a gestalt therapy framework. Initially the attention to creativity in psychotherapy writing is linked and focused on disorder or distress and the resultant healing effect of the creative process, for example art therapy. However there are so many fields of endeavor to which creativity is essential that we would be remiss in our therapeutic conceptualisations if we did not consider and include them. It is evident as with the quote from Mozart this existed long before psychotherapy and these wider fields offer us so much more understanding of the underlying workings of creativity. These descriptions of the creative process as worded so beautifully by Mozart have been given by many other artists and writers, modern and ancient. This includes Steven King (the horror story writer) who said jokingly in an interview that he didn't know where they ideas came from but he was worried if he didn't write them out he might do them. Actors also describe a similar process of creativity -

"Whether you are writing, singing painting or whatever, your objective is to feel liberated. So the less intellectual conscious thought that you are having at the time you are actually working, the better. You have to look for ways of elaborating, of expanding, of illuminating your imagination to get at that wellspring which is your unconscious.

In acting you are constantly trying to get out of the way and serve as a conduit to let this other person come through. That is a frustration because you are here and you do have that constant chatter of your intellect and you do have your own problems and joys, but what you really want to do is let those aspects of yourself go quite. You pray for that loss of consciousness because it is a great feeling."

Annette Bening

I have been collecting such quotes over the years and they all carry defining aspects in how they describe the creative process. These criteria are now for me the hallmark of creative experience. I am impressed that this has been so well described by the seminal text of gestalt therapy. This sets it apart from so many therapies, inviting the therapist to be "more than" a "therapist" and also an active participant in the living of life. So many therapies unfortunately espouse the "adult" frame (as described in the last chapter), with the resultant focus on "outcome" and "adaptation" and "control". This misses honoring the paradoxical achievement of awareness, process and dialogue, as so aptly described by Yontef (1983).

The Creative Void

A defining element of creative experience is that the person feels neither fully directive nor simply surrendering to the process but is, like the child, actively engaged yet aware of the "other" of the field they are in.

> "... that is they engage themselves, put forward their interests and skills and ... finally they do not cling to the interests as 'theirs'. In the excitement of the creative they come to a creative impartiality..."

> (Perls, Hefferline and Goodman, 1951, pg 359)

124

This creative impartiality is clear in each of the quotes so far. Mozart does not know where the thoughts come from and cannot take credit for them. Van Dusen cannot take full credit as they are a 'given', and Annette Bening talks of the liberation of getting out of her own way to access a greater wellspring of the 'other'. This process is reflected by the following famous actor:

"When I return home I do at least 90 minutes on my next script. I'm very methodical and get different coloured pens and mark each line. I number each line one to four as I learn them, putting an asterisk at each fifth line. I don't know why exactly but it seems to work. I go through the lines, perhaps twenty or thirty of them, again and again until I know them.

Then I start on the next set. But by then the words have started doing something in my subconscious and images appear. I know it sounds mad, but there's something whispering to me and I get a photographic image in my mind's eye of the guy I'm playing. For Hannibal Lecter I suddenly saw someone who had a round head and slicked back hair, who never blinks and moves like a cat."

Sir Anthony Hopkins

Many writers, philosophers, poets, artists, mystics and psychologists have sought to define and understand the creative process which in ancient times was attributed to a visitation from the Muses - the nine sister Goddesses, offspring of Zeus and Mnemosyne. These accounts of this process above give insight to the nature of creative genius, encourage humility in creative endeavors and can be seen in gestalt therapy within a field perspective lens which offers guidance and context for the trainee, student, therapist and trainer.

In our work as trainers (O'Neill and O'Neill, 2008) and in work in expanding and defining the Field Perspective (O'Neill and Gaffney, 2008) the simplest, most difficult and profoundly potent focus for the trainee gestalt therapist is being aware of the immediate contact and relationship which develops when they meet someone. We have termed this "being present to the creative emergence of the field" (O'Neill and Gaffney, 2008, O'Neill 2010). Much of this training with students over the four year program involves an encouragement to not be interested in fixing the problem the person presents with, but be involved in a more immediate exploration of what is happening for both the person and therapist as they explore why they have come to counselling and the present moment and the experience of being human. Of course the main reason acting from a 'middle mode' is so challenging for students is that they fear making mistakes, looking foolish, being confirmed they are dumb or unworthy, which as Perls, Hefferline and Goodman points out is the need for "security". The solution offered by gestalt therapy theory in PHG is to sacrifice this security for a state of "readiness" which is synonymous with the experiences of creativity and the 'middle mode'. This needs both the person coming to counselling as well as the therapist to be comfortable, or at least experimenting with tolerating the polarised opposites they are experiencing at times - which the Polsters (1999) define as 'point and counterpoint'.

The Creative Paradox of Point/Counterpoint

Another defining hallmark of the creative process is the person will be aware of (and even embrace) the paradoxes that present, and in therapy this is evident as a shift from an 'either/or' way of thinking and being to a 'both/and' experience of being. From both my grounding in gestalt therapy and through working in the drug and alcohol field, I have come to perceive that a healthy maturity for any person (organism) is marked by our ability to tolerate and even rejoice in our paradoxical nature as human beings. I notice people begin their counselling work in this area of substance abuse by trying to hide or negate the issue which plagues them such as

*I *want to use drugs/drink**

and instead try to change themselves by focusing on

I don't want to use drugs /drink.

There is a temptation for counsellors to support *I don't want to use/drink* and not attend to *I want to* use/drink. It is the attending to both, point and counterpoint, which is one of the key successes of the Motivational Interviewing interventions. Having been with many people as they struggle with such strongly polarised and powerful aspects of their nature, I believe a maturity and turning point is reached when someone says:

I would LOVE to drink or use drugs... AND I'm not going to.

The ethical attitude for counsellors is in listening to the whole person and attending to what's next, as opposed to simply trying to change people for the better with an outcome in mind. Of course this is easier said than done - we are human after all. Also I do not think such creative therapy approaches are solely within the realm of Gestalt therapy as I've met some excellent case managers in mental health/psychiatry who, whatever words they use to describe themselves and their theoretical approach, are working from the same perspective.

There is a significant overlap in the literature on case management, therapeutic alliance, recovery from mental illness and gestalt therapy in this area.

Creatively Authentic

I am interested to show the importance of utilising the wider field of our being in working with people in therapy. This is to encourage Gestalt therapy trainees to notice the shift from trying to be excessively in control of the therapy situation to being present and responding from the moment in the field...much the same as a skier or musician or actor would. As the Polsters note, this does not mean giving primacy to the spontaneous whims of the therapist, as "*spontaneity is no guarantee of excellence*". They define authenticity as 'responsible spontaneity' which is being authentic from a field perspective. This is where who we are is not only defined from our experience of "self-as-separate" but also from our experience as "self-in-the-field". This field perspective definition of self is one that identifies with our own spontaneous emerging figures and with the effect these responses have on the wider field. This a definition of is echoed by a few gestalt therapy writers -

"Free expression attains its fullest meaning primarily within the behavior which accepts responsibility for what follows"

Polster, E. & Polster, 1973. page 22

"The committed therapist has to know, but also must be able to control the expression of, his own impatience, his own ambition and competitiveness, his own anxiety. Voluntary commitment demands sacrifices, the giving up of interests and involvements of value for the dedication to a greater value. This is the most difficult aspect of commitment".

Laura Perls, 1991.page 226.

In the next chapter these aspects of the Creative found in Gestalt therapy will be developed further within the newly emerging 'field perspective' (O'Neill and Gaffney, 2008) and with reference to both paradoxical agency, emergent creation, and the beauty of poetry.

THE BIRTH OF SOLITUDE

At this heart-felt centre
Lies an aching need of Solitude
Cast into flesh
As I look into my little sons' eyes,
I know the worth of this bloodied birth.

The soul of spirit
different in connecting
to the heart of the father
and the heart of the son...

For when the veil of mortality melts
and figure returns to ground
I see the tree eternal,

And in that moment of eternal solitude
I no longer die each night.

Solitude gives birth and we are One.

K'un / The Receptive

"The Receptive is just as important as the Creative, but the attribute of devotion defines the the place occupied by this primal power in relation to the Creative.

For the Receptive must be activated and led by the Creative; then it is productive of good."

I-Ching, pg 11
Wilhelm, 1950

Being Present to the Emergent Creation of the Field: Wordsworth, Buber and Gestalt Therapy.

(Originally in Gestalt Review, 2010 and here with alterations)

Abstract

The field perspective in gestalt therapy remains a rich source of controversy and challenge in outlining and explaining a theory of practice. In teaching gestalt therapy, particularly the field perspective, it is useful to find examples of the principles which direct and support practice, as well as enhance and expand theory. Latner offers the field as an inspiring, evocative idea and suggests that when a term such as this has a connotative richness, we can best define it by searching for examples that "speak to us" (Latner, 2008). He offers how he is inspired by the writing of Dogen, a Zen

Buddhist teacher writing a thousand years ago, and how he intuitively understands a field universe through his writing. In a similar fashion, Martin

Buber and William Wordsworth speak with a connotative richness of *emergent creation* and *paradoxical agency*, two principles of the field perspective recently described in the literature (O'Neill & Gaffney, 2008). This article is an experiment in reaching out for just such connotative richness - an intuitive understanding of these two principles of field theory, *emergent creation* and *paradoxical agency*, to find an articulation of these principles in ways that speak to gestalt practitioners.

"While with an eye made quiet by the power
Of harmony, and with deep power of joy,
We see into the life of things."

(Wordsworth, *Lines Composed a Few Miles Above Tintern Abbey, On Re-visiting the Banks of the Wye During a Tour, June 13, 1798*, pgs 104-105)

There are blessed moments in the life of every gestalt therapist where they experience in their work a sense of ease, of fluidity, of being attuned to the moment and the context of existence. At such moments the more directive, goal oriented aspects of the self are *"made quiet"* and out of the chaos of our work with individuals, couples, families, groups, organizations and even communities, a world of harmony becomes clear. Such moments are manifest and manifold in the arts. We are no longer playing violin solo but are part of the orchestra and music; as a painter we sense the painting is painting us; and we are so well rehearsed in the play that something more than the words come through and we surf the wave of this new creation. Such experiences are often joyful, and bring an expanded sense of self and other, so *"we see into the life of things"*.

As all students of gestalt therapy would know, the journey to these blessed states of being take many years and it is with furtive longing that we view the work of experienced practitioners and trainers, and with painful, at times shameful, exasperation that we struggle to match the seeming effortless wisdom of these masters. As all trainers and supervisors know, such obvious skill only comes through years of ardent work and of learning from our mistakes, and it is with an eventual humble surrender to principles of life greater than those our ego would prefer, that allows us to reap the rewards of practice, practice, practice.

The work of a trainer, supervisor or mentor, while guided by similar principles to that of the practitioner, is also importantly different. While both the practice and teaching of gestalt rests in gestalt therapy as a philosophy of being, the way in which these principles are lived in teaching is important to distinguish from practice. For example, Tiger Woods may be a great golfer but he goes to a golf coach to help him improve his game, as there are different skills and attitudes required in the "preparing for doing" compared to the "doing". Each of course is a form of "doing" yet the work of preparation, of training, supervising and mentoring is a learning process which may pass on knowledge and even understanding, but cannot, as again trainers and supervisors know, pass on the "lived wisdom" where practitioners allows the efforts of their ego to *"go quiet"* and surrender to the *"power of Harmony"* and thus "see into the life of things".

As described elsewhere (Levine Bar Yoseph et al, 2008) training gestalt therapists has received little attention in the literature. In part this may be because of the challenge in passing on more than the basic skills of counseling and psychotherapy (to which less holistic approaches are agreeable) and the gestalt approach requires a more complex articulation of that which is a "lived wisdom.

Added to this challenge is the complexity of the initial text itself (Perls et al, 1951) and the controversy of the field perspective in gestalt therapy, which has been described as difficult and demanding (Yontef, 1993) and which has tended to divide into two camps of those who prefer the work of Levine and those who eschew this for the foundational "organism/environment field" of Perls et al. This initial conceptualization of the organism/environment field of Perls, Hefferleine and Goodman (1951) is complex in its simplicity. It presents as an amalgam of esoteric writing, social critique, psychoanalytical terminology and practical exercises on awareness and contact. Since it was written there have been notable developments in gestalt therapy literature to refine or better describe field theory and link theory to practice (Latner, 1983; Yontef, 1993; Parlett, 1993, 1997, 2005; Staemmler, 2006; O'Neill, 2008).

More recently O'Neill and Gaffney (2008) present an integrative articulation of these two field theories in gestalt therapy and apply this conceptualization to therapy with a case study, describing the philosophy and principles of field theory in practice. In this previous work, rather than describing this as field *theory*, this is denoted as a field *perspective* and there is presented a heuristic list of principles which guide practice (common to all field theory approaches) and suitable for application in gestalt therapy research. They have termed this integrative view of field theory as the "*field perspective*" to note it is wider than a single theory alone and that it includes the main elements and commonalities of these theories as applicable to our practice as therapists, as well as trainers.

The One Field in Practice

It is the intention of this current chapter to thus further explore two of these principles of a field perspective, both from an integrative view of field theory and more importantly to explore a creative way to support training and practice of gestalt therapy. Hence rather than being a further critique of field theory, the purpose will be simply to extend and expand on this field perspective by attending in more detail to two of these principles. The two principles which will be addressed are precisely those which attend to the struggle of trainees and trainers alike, as mentioned above, which require a degree of surrender of the ego to a wider process in the field while paradoxically and intentionally making use of this expanded awareness as a therapist. These two principles have been described as *Paradoxical Agency* and *Emergent Creation.* It is also the intention of this article to explore these field perspective principles by using other creative sources and writings which "speak to" these principles which more poetically voice that which traditional theory cannot help leave a little dry. The examples which most speak to the author are those of Wordsworth and Buber.

As a reader please note the shift as we move from theoretical articulation to the poetry and back, and how each informs you in its own way. I would suggest for its fuller impact, and to allow the poetry to be appreciated in its own form, that you might consider reading aloud with a pace which allows the grace of the work to speak to you. I hope this will support moving between the theory and the poetry, as one might in actual therapy when we find ourselves moving between being present in the moment and at times reflecting and thinking about the process. This thus also demonstrates an alternative teaching method, of using literature or music or art to "inspire" us and remind us of those experiences which do not dwell in the heady world of theory alone which I hope enhance and delight our theoretical musing and direct our choice as we practice theoretical principles, to the stage where practice becomes lived authentic being.

This approach of using wider sources than the traditional theory of therapy is discussed by Latner (2008) who described the field as an inspiring, evocative idea which is best thought of as an attitude. He critiques attempts to describe the field as a theory, a rigorous set of interlocking ideas, and prefers to define it as an "evocative field perspective" from which he derives a "constellation of ideas that come out of field thinking" (Latner, 2008, pg 27).Both Latner and O'Neill & Gaffney coalesce in their writing on the importance of creativity in describing the field in gestalt therapy. As Latner states –

> *"The field is an encompassing pregnancy, a potentiality that becomes actual and takes a specific form from contact. Its nature is spontaneous and ephemeral; its form is fluid, continuously created and recreated."*
>
> *(*Latner, 2008, pg 24 *)*

Emergent Creation

O'Neill and Gaffney note that while creativity has been given attention in Gestalt therapy it has not been well defined from a field perspective. They describe creativity from a field perspective as "emergent creation", a figure/ground formation in the field as a whole, in comparison to an experience of creation from an individualistic paradigm, (which

151

includes the co-creation of both individuals together). They propose that emergent creation is a process whereby a figure emerges from the greater whole and, as such, is different and more than the sum of the creations of each part. This is a creation from the field without individual agency or intention – a holistic paradigm of creation as compared to an individualistic one.

In essence, this equates to the agency of the whole towards the parts as aptly defined by Wertheimer when describing the field perspective in Gestalt psychology, when he states –

> *"There are wholes, the behavior of which is not determined by that of their individual elements, but where the part-processes are themselves determined by the intrinsic nature of the whole"*

> (Wertheimer, 1925 in Ellis 1938, p. 2)

This principle in which a whole determines the behavior of the individual parts is more common place than it might at first seem. It is particularly prevalent in everyday life, where individuals are part of a team and they become swept into the synergy of the functioning of the team – such as with a sporting team, an orchestra or band, a choir, a emergency team in a hospital, a family and community. Even with individual pursuits in arts, theatre, sports, and drama, the combined experience of the performer and the audience can come together to create an experience (or figure) which emerges creatively from the whole and is not dependant on the performer.

In therapy the authors describe this creative process as a figure which emerged from the field of the implicit reality (or implicate order) of the client/therapist field (O'Neill & Gaffney, 2008) and so to discriminate this from other creations which are more explicitly individually co-created, they chose the term emergent creation in that it is created and emerges from the implicate order of the field.

In the previous work Gaffney describes working with a client involved with three men. He notices that when he mentions one she has a pattern of mentioning the others as well. He notes this as a figural pattern in *her* field or life space. He later notices how she looks at him at times and this reminds him of his father when he was angry.

Eventually he risks sharing this and she tells him this does not apply to her. This figure has emerged from *his* field or life space. Later in another session he keeps getting images of gloves and sees no pattern of sense to this in either his or her field. As the image is repetitive he trusts this might have meaning and shares it with her, tentatively. She becomes emotional and relates how when she was young her parents bought her woolen gloves which itched and no matter how often she would lose them they were replaced. She had no choice. Now she was an adult she could afford as many pairs of gloves as she wanted and had a rich collection at home to choose from. This connects with her current difficulty in choice of the men. The figure though has somehow emerged from the wider field of the therapist client dyad and is more than just the field or life space of one or the other. It is a figure which connects both in someway and arises beyond the simple individualistic logic of the separate egos and life spaces. As we stated previously, the process whereby an event of the client's past emerged as an image in the therapist and returned to the client is the magic and the mystery of a field approach. While there is no doubt that the process of the gloves image can be, or soon will be, open to a generally acceptable "scientific" explanation, our interest is not in such an explanation as we are more concerned with the experience of this process and its value in a therapeutic setting.

Surrendering to Paradoxical Agency

Such concepts of reality as emergent creation are challenging to students and practitioners of gestalt therapy. To accept and work as a therapist from this principle of emergent creation requires a degree of surrender by the student or therapist. O'Neill and Gaffney title this "surrender to paradoxical agency" and describe how in Gestalt therapy, as opposed to other schools, we do not try to measure or "control" the individual as a separate phenomenon.

The field perspective consists of being aware and attuned to the operation of the contact boundary in the organism/environment field, rather than satisfying the need for the therapist to exercise control of the therapeutic situation as in some approaches. That is easier said than done of course, for a student or beginning therapist who is doing their best to apply the theory to practice, and therefore "trying" to exert some form of control over what is happening.

In part, the challenge of allowing and working with emergent creation is a paradoxical process of searching for balance between willful choice and acceptance of what "is" for both the therapist and client. This is described in the original text of Perls et al (1951) as the middle mode - the space between active and passive functioning, where the person is accepting, attending and growing into the solution, with the substitution of readiness (or faith) for the security of apparent control (Perls, Hefferline and Goodman, 1951).

The original text of Perls et al (1951) asks therapists, from a field perspective, to have faith in something more than their individual agency, to let go of their need for security and control and instead to be present in the moment – to be present to the emergent creation of the field.

This *readiness* of middle mode described by Perls et al (1951) offers a paradoxical agency to the therapist - an ability to sense and chose being "in control" by surrendering control. They equate this state to one which is more familiar to children and artists, and indeed examples of such paradoxical agency are found aplenty in the arts, music and poetry, such as in the work of William Wordsworth. It is also a state frequently referred to by people who describe spiritual experiences, such a Martin Buber.

In teaching gestalt therapy, particularly the field perspective, it is useful to find examples of the principles which direct and support practice, as well as enhance and expand theory. Latner states that when a term has a connotative richness, we define it by searching for examples that "speak to us" (Latner, 2008). He gives the example of how he is inspired by the writing of Dogen, a Zen Buddhist teacher writing a thousand years ago, an how he intuitively "understands how to think about a field-universe in which each being construes his/her reality as universal" (Latner, 2008, pg 25).

In a similar fashion, Martin Buber and William Wordsworth speak with a *connotative richness* about creative emergence and paradoxical agency. So it is in reaching out for an intuitive understanding and enrichment of emergent creation and paradoxical agency that we now turn to Wordsworth and Buber for articulation of these principles of a field perspective. Wordsworth's poetry is popular with many, and in particular he speaks to those who have loosened the bonds of what Charles Tart refers to as Ordinary Waking

Consciousness (Tart, 1975), allowing perception and awareness to expand beyond normal everyday affairs. In his poem *Lines Composed a Few Miles Above Tintern Abbey, On Re-visiting the Banks of the Wye During a Tour, June 13, 1798*, Wordsworth describes being neither totally directive nor passive –

"That blessed mood,
In which the burden of the mystery,
In which the heavy and the weary weight
Of all this unintelligible world,
Is lightened: - that serene and blessed mood,
In which the affection gently lead us on, -
Until the breath of this corporeal frame
And even the motion of our human blood
Almost suspended, we are laid asleep
In body and become a living soul;
While with an eye made quiet by the power
Of harmony, and with deep power of joy,
We see into the life of things."

(Wordsworth, 1798, (1950), pgs 104-105)

Some may at first draw back and wonder at the relevance of this esoteric and mystical language to the practice of gestalt therapy, yet consider the struggles of Goodman in Perls et al (1951) in finding ways to describe similar states of being such as middle mode. This is so when describing the 'Id' state, which reads in a similar fashion, in part, to that described by Wordsworth. Perls et al (1951) used poetic language similar to Wordsworth at times, several times mentioning the "soul" and discuss the nature of poetry and its importance as a language for reality.

Martin Buber, in a similar fashion, is not shy to leap into script which might leave the uninitiated reader behind -

"The fiery stuff of all my ability to will seethes tremendously, all that I might do circles around me, still without actuality in the world, flung together and seemingly inseparable, alluring

glimpses of powers flicker from all the uttermost bonds; the universe is my temptation, and I achieve being in an instant, with both hands plunged deep into the fire, where the single deed is hidden, the deed which aims at me – now is the moment!"

(Buber, 1958, pg 51-52)

With these words Buber describes the shift from a reign of causality in the world of It, where every event and experience is either caused or causing, to the world of relation, where the I and Thou "freely confront one another in mutual effect, that is neither connected with, nor colored by, causality."

He defines the nature and stance of the paradoxical agency of the therapist poetically, when he avows that destiny and freedom are "promised to each other." By this he means there is a choice in acceptance of "what is" rather than aiming for control of the situation, as promised by the perspective of causality. He describes

162

this poetically and paradoxically as the "deed which aims at me". He goes on to describe how such a state is only available to those who have the freedom given by knowing relationship and the presence of Thou.

Poetic Practice

It is the task of the trainer and supervisor to envisage ways to create a setting which, though structured, provides the safety and stage in which the trainee can justifiable let go a little of the need for control and allow themselves to be in the moment. One such exercise developed in training at the Illawarra Gestalt Centre has been borrowed from work with Frank Farrelly (who developed Provocative Therapy) and Steve Brigham. It has three steps or stages. Trainees begin by sitting in dyads and we explore first how each person prepares themselves to be less distracted and more present. The first experience then involves one person taking the time to be in a state where they feel ready and then at this point they signal the other person to begin talking. As the second person talks the "job" of the first person is to sit silently attuned to the other.

This first part is usually challenging as students who are being silent and centered want to show in all variety of ways that they are, indeed, attending and so some vigorously nod and signal to do so. The result, as they discuss afterwards, is that paradoxically such concerns reduce their sense of being present, both for them and the other person. Yet this now offers the student and practitioner a choice in awareness of being as doing, and not needing to do for the sake of doing.

The next step in the experience is for the silent person to now talk when they want to and to allow this to emerge from whatever takes their own fancy, irrelevant to the person opposite them. Therefore as an example the trainer may show how to talk *'gobbledygook '* and speak in word salad.

This experience is freeing for some and alternatively unbearable for others who hold a need to be the "good attentive" therapist and once again, when discussed afterwards, brings fruitful discussions around the balance of excessively attending versus relaxing into a spontaneous space.

The final phase of the experience involves the person now being centered and present, as well as sensing their ability to be spontaneous and then using this therapeutically. In this instance the spontaneous responses which are invited are the various images which arise for the therapist. They are thus able to practice being spontaneous therapeutically by sharing whatever images come into their head while the other person talks. They are encouraged to trust in the image and share it (and not further explain it) for the other person. The result is that they experience these images arising spontaneously and outside their ego control, and the person talking begins to make meaning from the images. As with reflective listening, the images may be changed by the person talking and that is also encouraged as a co-created field. One might say "as you talk about your work, I get the sudden image of a cage" and the person may say "well it is but I am aware the door of the cage is open."

This experience also brings both therapist and client outside of the world of "talking about" the issues and more actively accessing a richer language of experience of imagery, similar to that of poetry. In such moments the barrier of talk can dissolve into a mutuality that is evident in the case study above with the image of the gloves which is described by both Buber and Wordsworth.

Wordsworth, like Buber, had a knowing relationship with the presence of Thou, and this appears time and again in his poetry.

In the Womb we know the Universe, In Birth we forget it.

This state of being the poet and mystic describe, a state open to emergent creation and accepting paradoxical agency, is seen by both Wordsworth and Buber to be a faculty that already exists and is found by un-learning as much as by new learning. Both are clear that such states of being and awareness are available but have been "lost" by a process of psychological "development".

As described previously (Chapter 2. The Rediscovery of Childhood) Buber presents developmental stages which show the transition from the life in the womb, which is cosmic in nature, to life in the world of 'It'. The first stage of this development is also a loss, as described in the mystical

Jewish saying "in the mother's body man knows the universe, in birth he forgets it", and so is this initial experience of birth a loss as well as a gain.

This change that is happening, unlike the physical birth itself, is not a sudden one but gradual – "time is granted to the child to exchange a spiritual connexion, *relation,* for the natural connection with the world that he gradually loses." (Buber, 1958, pg, 25)

In a strikingly similar manner to Buber's developmental devolution, Wordsworth describes this evolution and paradoxical devolution of the child into the adult in the poem *Intimations of Immortality from Recollections of Early Childhood,* (William Wordsworth, 1950, pgs 542 -543)

In this poem, similar to Buber, he provides a model of human development which portrays the early years of childhood through to adulthood as one of spiritual devolution or un-development. The child begins "trailing clouds of glory" as with Buber's description of the cosmic nature and awareness in the womb. Wordsworth almost shouts the next developmental stage – "Heaven lies about us in our infancy!" and Buber describes this as the infant's instinct is to make everything into a Thou (Buber, 1958, pg 27).

With both Buber and Wordsworth the stages into adulthood are irrevocably contained in the metaphor of light, or its loss, as with the next stage of being a boy, which is to experience "Shades of the prison house" while still beholding the light and by the stage of being a Youth is still attended by "the vision splendid". It is the man to whom this cosmic inscape dies, as this initial expanded awareness fades "into the light of common day" – the common light of Buber's world of I-It and Causality.

Buber is more paradoxical and apposite in

his use of light as a metaphor, yet conveys the same meaning when he states "He (the child) has stepped out of the glowing darkness of chaos into the cool light of creation." (Buber, 1958, pg 25) How sad if that was the end of our developmental process. Yet it is at this point when we reach our mature state as physical and psychological beings that Buber tells how there is a call to return to the initial experiences of the states of awareness and for childhood to re-emerge for the adult.

Buber speaks of this developmental process as a movement, like a tidal force, in which the relation of Thou, which the child is born from, gives birth, as it were, to the experience of I. This is a movement, not linear, back and forward, between a sense of relation and a return to the cool light of creation. In this tidal process of back and forth the "I" grows stronger and becomes conscious of "I". As this happens the discrimination of "not I" also develops, so

"The man who has become aware of I, that is I-It, stands before things but not over against them in the flow of mutual action" (Buber 1958 pg 29).

From this stance of I-It the person takes possession of all It and objectifies things with the magnifying glass of observation and the field glasses of remote inspection. In such existential isolation lies the aloneness of the modern world – the person detached from universality and uniqueness. This allows for the co-ordination and causal control of these objects, and the desired security of the illusion of control.

A World that is ordered is not the World Order.

Yet this cool light of creation, this age of Causality, is not the end point. As Buber states in iconoclastic brevity – "a world that is ordered, is not the world order." (Buber, pg 31) The world of relation, the world of

Thou, calls out with a note as the individual stands fully present in the world order.

> *"These moments are immortal, and most transitory of all; no content may be secured from them, but their power invades creation and the knowledge of man, beams of their power stream into the ordered world and dissolve it again and again."*
>
> (Buber, 1958 pg 31)

All are affected by this call, this note, in one way or another. It may be through illness or death, through a gentle change in life, through marriage or child rearing, or in the pursuit of what one loves doing best.

Whatever way it happens the note is sounded and I-It begins to dissolve in respect for the experience of the world of relation. This is the emergent creation of the field. Such experiences challenge and deconstruct the world of Causality and the illusion of control, and demand an acceptance of the paradoxical nature of the agency of the field – of which all are a part.

Some, like Wordsworth, hear this note relatively early, are ready and respond. Most struggle and move back and forward between the coordinated world of order and the relational world order of Thou that surrounds us. Some fight the experience and the stronger the note and the stronger the fight, the greater the illness or dis-order that results.

Today many people cling to the world order, get lost in the appearance of job success, of financial security or any of the treasures which attach so easily. Others turn the call into a battle with their demons, or the demons of other people, and miss the "clouds of glory" in the battle. Many people try to sedate the call with drugs or alcohol or food - feeding the physical self until it weights down the 'I-Thou' with its gravity of biological processes. These experiences, these struggles, this sense of loss of order, control and 'Causality' is experienced as a dis-order. The rise of the professional mental health worker and counsellor have created a workforce which often is a part of the institutions of order and seek to help the individual reduce the experience of dis-order and restore order once more.

Like religion in the past, psychotherapy has developed as a social endeavour to assist in finding order for those who are experiencing these struggles of disorder.

Already the potential trap of therapy becomes obvious. If it does not have the ability to transcend the institutionalised world of Causality, therapy itself becomes part of the problem. It is as an alternative to this trap that gestalt therapy and other approaches developed, and it is the field perspective principles such as emergent creation and paradoxical agency which articulate principles to guide this work.

At first people enter the therapy process due to struggling with the lack of order and to try to gain control again. Many therapies have been developed to support this aim. Yet the nature of gestalt therapy, instead of offering control over the experienced symptoms, is to heighten awareness, contact and dialogue with the faith that through being present to "what is", change happens.

This change is a developmental change, not a cure for an ill, and from Buber's perspective we enter again, more and more, into the world of relation, of I-Thou. As both therapists and clients learn, or un-learn, to open to and be present to emergent creation with a sense of paradoxical agency, then a change happens in how they view the world and others. Wordsworth and Buber both note the significant impact this has on relationships in the world – not only with people but also with nature, such as trees and daffodils. Buber talks of how a tree can be looked at - as a picture, perceived as a movement, classified as a species, subdued in actual presence so it is viewed as an expression of a biological law, and even scattered in number, by counting it as one of many. In all these contacts the tree remains an object.

Yet if he becomes "bound up in relationship to it" the tree is no longer an "It" and he becomes seized by the power of its exclusiveness - a mutuality of I-Thou, the tree itself (Buber, pg 7-8). The tree is no longer only an It to be numbered, classified or viewed (like clients can be also) and is experienced more fully and mutually *in relationship*.

This attitude and experience teaches and hopefully inspires us to remember such mutuality in mental health care and therapy. While assessment and diagnosis have an important role to play, they become full as we also preserve and live the relationship with the "other". Like Buber, this wealth of relationship with nature is abundant in the poetry of Wordsworth. His poem that begins with "I wandered lonely as a cloud" tells of this I-Thou relationship with a hill of daffodils He extends this relation with nature and his environment even more so to the city of London.

The poem, "Composed Upon Westminster Bridge, Sept, 3rd, 1802", offers a view of the city early in the morning where Wordsworth senses the very life of the city itself, at a time when the air was still clean and the city flowed easily into the surrounding countryside, long before the congestion, smog and pollution of today.

> *"Earth has not anything to show more fair:*
> *Dull would he be of soul who could pass by*

A sight so touching in its majesty:
This City doth, like a garment, wear
The beauty of the morning, silent, bare,
Ships, towers, domes, theatres, and
temple lie
Open unto the fields, and to the sky;
All bright and glittering in the
smokeless air.
Never did sun more beautifully steep
In his first splendour, valley, rock or
hill;
Ne'er saw I, never felt, a calm so deep!
The river glideth at his own sweet will;
Dear God! The very houses seem
asleep;
And all that mighty heart is lying still!"

Wordsworth, *Composed Upon*
Westminster Bridge, Sept, 3rd, 1802

It is this relation to our environment, this movement to I-Thou with nature and animals, that has inspired the work of organisations such as Greenpeace and the politics of ecology which seek to avert the impact of a world used from an I-It stance - to more readily embrace a relationship with our environment, with the greater whole of which all are part. Our world today is, perhaps more than any other time, impacted by our ability to control so many processes through technology and science.

This approach to making use of technologies has also carried over into health care and therapy, so the application of techniques and modalities is valued, at times rightly so. However it is in balance to this technological ability that an appreciation of emergent creation and paradoxical agency stands out as being so necessary and important.

Like the poetry of Wordsworth and the writing of Buber, gestalt therapy stands out as a field perspective which allows and enlarges to include the wider environment, "A sight so touching in it majesty."

To Conclude

This wider connection with the greater whole is in part the intention of this article – to inspire therapists and trainers to reach for writing and experiences outside of the traditional therapeutic writing – to find poetry and prose which speak to them with beauty and embolden therapists to surrender to the paradoxical agency of the emergent creation of the field. There is nothing as useful as a good theory, and as teachers aspire to encourage a theory of practice, then ethically what happens is training and practice is guided by principles, which in turn based on coherent theory.

At the same time, there is learning beyond traditional theory which comes from experience and a way of being in the world. This requires a different approach to learning, both are valid, and the more intuitive learning is often found in creative pursuits and in poetry, music, drama, and the visual arts. This article tries to offer a path of learning in the field perspective by reaching out for an intuitive understanding in the work of Wordsworth and Buber, who provide an articulation of these principles of emergent creation and paradoxical agency.

This chapter offers an experiment in finding other sources of to encourage the reader, as trainer and therapist, to consider the potential for examining their relationship with the greater whole, as described in the theoretical statement of Wertheimer. To find examples of the principles which direct and support training and practice with a connotative richness by searching for examples that "speak to us" and support how we intuitively understands how to live such principles as emergent creation and paradoxical agency. To inspire them to move with Buber's tidal wash between the world of Causality and the world of relation, between a world that is ordered and the

World Order, and experience the risk of occasionally surrendering to discovering the intrinsic nature of the whole, of which all are a part.

STIRRINGS

I am massaged
by the sound of the air
through the pine and eucalypt trees
The sound tells of sunny winter days
And the crisp smell of snow on alpine hills
And monks and nuns
In gentle prayer.
With a longing beyond time
And my soul smells the fresh air
While my brain unknowing
Considers psychiatric curriculum
On a computer screen.
I adjust the chair
to sit with an upright back,
not slouching
A martial artist in horse stance
where the true art of war
Is the common, everyday
Attendance
To the
Sound of the wind
In the pine and eucalypts

Chun / Difficulty at the Beginning

"...in the chaos of difficulty at the
beginning,
order is already implicit.
In order to find one's place in the
infinity of being,
one must be able both to separate and
to unite"

I-Ching, pg 17
Wilhelm, 1950

Spirituality, Physics and the Poetry of Gestalt therapy

"To see a world in a grain of sand,
And a heaven in a wild flower,
Hold infinity in the palm of your hand,
And eternity in an hour."

Auguries of Innocence
William Blake

From my previous writing on the application of physics and quantum physics to psychotherapy (O'Neill 2008, O'Neill 2012) I want to now conclude by joining my previous musings on physics with ideas that connect with creativity, the recollection of childhood and spirituality. It may seem a broad brush to wield, yet I remain fascinated by the likenesses I find in reading poetry, psychotherapy and physics.

In particular the work of David Bohm (1993) in his book *The Undivided Universe* offers conceptualization and metaphor from quantum physics which translate well to psychotherapy, spirituality and the Tao. The early quantum physicists Bohr (1961), and Heisenberg saw that awareness was a priori a part of this everyday Classical reality and so they needed to include awareness as part of the quantum equation (Lightman, 2000).

Bohm extended this perspective by offering a holographic description of reality. The hologram produces a three dimensional image by splitting and reunifying light and this offers a conceptual model for how the brain "creates" reality and how each part of a reality contains the whole. What interested Bohm was the hologram does not look like the object but creates an image when it is illuminated by a laser beam. It produces another order of wholeness, which he saw as "enfolded" or "implicit" within the form. So the hologram is enfolded and implicate order (invisible reality) and this can be unfolded to produce an explicate order (visible reality).

In re-reading the poetry quote at the beginning by Blake, we can hear him both as poet and mystic describing this same process as Bohm long before the arrival of quantum physics. Poetry precedes physics.

This process of enfoldment and unfoldment of physical and non-physical reality (whether we call it quantum or spiritual) as described by both William Blake and David Bohm correspond to the laws of quantum reality and the shifts between classical reality and quantum reality through awareness

The second phenomenon which interested Bohm was an apparatus made of two concentric glass cylinders with a viscous liquid between the outer and inner cylinder. Into the fluid is put a drop of insoluble ink.

When the cylinder is rotated the ink spreads out into a thread and eventually disappears. However when the order is reversed and the cylinder rotated back the ink droplet reappears. Hence while it looks like there is no visible order once it has disappeared, there is obviously, like the hologram, some order otherwise the droplet could not reform.

When a series of droplets are used then the order between them at first seems not to exist yet as they enfold and unfold it becomes clear they are linked in some way by an implicate order. Bohm and Hiley (1993) state that an event thus is only "actual" or observable to us as it unfolds into manifest reality, yet it is always present whether unfolded or not.

In short what is exciting about this to the gestalt therapist is Bohm is describing the awareness process of figure/ground and organism/environment field. Admittedly this is not clear at first as he is using the language of quantum physics and not psychotherapeutic language. This has been noted earlier in the same context of mystical and spiritual language with psychotherapy and how with some patience the links between the two fields can become apparent. If we use our ability, as Jung describes, to enter both aspects of a paradox – to hold a "both/and" perspective of our own ideas as well as those of others the links across these different fields can appear.

Looking with Soft Eyes

As a practical example, in teaching field perspectives in our training program (O'Neill and O'Neill 2008) we show students those books of pictures where at first each picture looks like a jumbled chaos of colours from which, when they learn to soften and de-focus their gaze, a three-dimensional image appears (The Magic Eye). The "trick" is to learn to look with "soft eyes" and out of chaos can appear harmony, with both "realities" being true for the observer. (You can view these images on their web site at http://www.magiceye.com/)

In a similar way Bohm (1993) states the perceived classical world is a result of each mind, aware of only a small part of the whole. The illusory aspect is believing that this part IS the whole, as when we believe the jumble of colours is all there is, as that is all we can see. When the classical world is perceived as a facet, then there is no illusion. So as therapists, the ability to "soften" our gaze to perceive other realities simultaneously becomes important.

Specifically individual identity as described by Bohm's idea of implicate order and the holomovement, is a clear parallel to the process of figure/ground and the gestalt therapy theory of the self. He notes the concept of a permanent entity with a given identity (self) is at best an approximation (illusion) whether this is as a particle or a person. This is similar to writing in PHG which states:

> "*Where the organism is mobile in a great field and has a complicated internal structure, like an animal, it seems plausible to speak of it by itself— as, for instance, the skin and what is contained in it–but this is simply an **illusion** due to the fact the motion through space and the internal detail call attention to themselves against the relative stability and simplicity of the background.*"
>
> (Perls, Hefferline and Goodman
> 1951, pg 228)

The experience of separateness in experiencing the self as illusory or an 'appearance of reality', or at best built on the functioning of a separate ego-sense of self that develops later in life and follows from the earlier models of development described previously through reference to Wordsworth, Buber and Perls, Hefferline and Goodman. As Buber writes, again echoing this wider idea of identity of Bohm:

"The human being is not a He or She, bounded from every other He or She, a specific point in space and time within the net of the world; nor is he a nature able to be experienced and described, a loose bundle of named qualities. But with no neighbour and whole in himself, he is Thou and fills the universe."

(Buber,1958, pg 8)

Physics and the *Bhagavad Gita*

There are similar correspondences to be found in reading the classic Hindu text, the Bhagavad Gita. In chapter 13 which deals with the Field and the Knower we read the following in the conversation between Arjuna and Krisna:

Arjuna: "I wish to learn about Prakriti and Brahmam, the Field and the Knower"

To understand these terms of Field (Prakriti) and the Knower of the Field (Brahmam) it helps to know that in Hinduism the same words are used at different levels and the reader must understand and be acting within the context of the level spoken about to know which meaning of the word is being used. To begin with Khrisna says clearly –

"The body is called the Field because a man sows seeds of action in it and reaps their fruits. Wise men say that the Knower of the Field is he who watches what takes place within the body."

In the literal sense Khrisna is explaining to Arjuna proposals remarkably similar to those put forward by Merleau-Ponty who describes a "lived-through-world". In the *Bhagavad Gita* the body plays a vital part (the fulfilment of the concept a la Husserl's idea of giving flesh to a concept by realizing it in concrete terms.) So this first definition of Field is at the personal, or the *phenomenal field.*

Next Khrisna takes a leap and having defined the personal he jumps to Brahmam, the Absolute –

"Recognise me as the Knower of the Field in everybody"

This statement by Khrisna describes the transcendental field (Merleau-Ponty) or transcendental phenomenology (Husserl) and transcendental philosophy (Kant) and to give it the original meaning of the term – the transcendent. Hindu philosophy here offers a bridge between the knowable and the unknowable, and at this level Brahman (The Knower) is now no longer man as described within Western philosophical approaches as the knower of knowledge, but is now Brahmam and Prakriti (or Maya) who is now all mind and matter – the Field in a much wider sense, akin to physics.

Once again we note Blake's poetry says this at the beginning of the chapter, and in four deeply simple lines.

In a lecture in 1844 on the nature of atoms, Faraday made a bold leap of imagination and, like the shift we just saw Khrina offer to Arjuna, he turned the nature of reality away from the personal to the universal.

He proposed that, rather than seeing atoms as physical objects which give off a web of force, that perhaps the web of force itself was the reality and the atom existed as a concentration in that web of force. He then used a thought experiment to describe this. He asked the audience to imagine the Sun sitting in space by itself. What would happen if the Earth suddenly appeared in

199

its place? How would the Sun know it was there? He then said that before the Earth appeared the web of forces associated with the Sun – the field – is spread throughout space and so as soon as the Earth appeared it would have an impact on this field of force. This impact on the field would tell the Earth the Sun existed – therefore the Field is the reality the Earth experiences, not the Sun itself.

Faraday argued that these lines or webs of force filled the universe and is the reality by which these seemingly separate entities are connected. A Field perspective indeed! So Faraday describes the material world of atoms and suns as being like "knots" in the various fields of force. For Hinduism, individuals are similarly like "knots" of being in the reality of Brahmam.

If we look with 'soft eyes' this is remarkably similar to what Perls, Hefferline and Goodman say about reality, self and organism-environment field. We are a "system of contacts" (knots) in the organism/environment field (Brahman). Einstein took this further with combining matter and energy so both were not either "knots" of the field they were in, but both - a both/and perspective.

Dialogical Physics: The Poetry of Martin Buber.

When we read Buber we can similarly translate what he is writing to the frame of physics, poetry and he lives in the world of the mystic. For example in correspondence with what Faraday says above, Buber states it this way –

> *"The world of It is set in the context of space and time. The world of Thou is not set in either of these... there exists the unbroken world of Thou: the isolated moments of relations are bound up in a life of world solidarity"*
>
> (Buber,1958, pg 8)

Therefore the world of 'It' is one of atoms and suns, which seem separate, yet the field perspective world of 'Thou', like quantum reality, is the underlying web of force (Faraday) which connects everything and is essentially the reality that is experienced.

> *"The human being is not a He or She, bounded from every other He or She, a specific point in space and time within the net of the world; nor is he a nature able to be experienced and described, a loose bundle of named qualities. But with no neighbour and whole in himself, he is Thou and fills the universe."*
>
> (Buber,1958, pg 8)

Considering the Bhagavad Gita, Buber, Bohm and Perls, Hefferline and Goodman as an example, we can stay with the meaning of a word such as "field", within a context (ie the personal) and rather than reduce its meaning by considering other contexts and meanings one can be aware of levels of connected meaning between each of these sources of writing and find where each appropriately may connect and support the other.

It is in the use of only ONE of these levels of meaning to describe everything that the problems occur – ie the "Reality Fight" that Latner (2008) writes about. If I am not trying to reduce all meaning to one level but instead am open with 'soft eyes' to explore, connect and learn from a stairway of meaning then this has the opposite effect to the reality fight.

By our being open to physics, poetry and spirituality as aspects of the organism/environment field in general and Gestalt therapy in particular we can be in accord with the early founders of gestalt therapy and embrace a "unitary approach" Hopefully we do this as children and artists with our soft eyes at work creatively and authentically in the present moment with each other.

"It is the sage of Tao that is 'like water', assuming the form of the receptacle. The increment of growth and learning, after good contact is certain, but it is small. The self has found and made its reality, but recognising what it has assimilated it sees it again as part of a vast field."

(Perls, Hefferline and Goodman
1951, pg 427)

"Therefore the sage puts his self last
yet his self is first
He treats his self as extraneous,
yet his self is preserved
Because he is without selfishness
his self can fully develop

(Tao Te Ching
Lao Tzu, page 32)

Epilogue

A Presence that Disturbs Me with Joy

The antidote to both these extremes that we discussed in the Prologue, to lose one self and to find oneself - the nihilism of "no self" or the "self is the all"- is again a Middle Way which transcends either alternative path. In this case the Middle way in found through holding the paradox of losing self to find self, of being void while still conscious, of being an owner of no-thing and no-self - while realising the closer one comes to being the Lord's the closer one is one's own self (Swedenborg, *Divine Providence*, 1764)

Several themes emerge from this discussion. First, there are issues of language and culture. Some words in mystical and religious texts do not readily translate to psychological texts such as with

Perls, Hefferline and Goodman and the teaching of Taoism, so we must involve ourselves in the frame of reference of the writings. Second, each writer is using words to translate an experience. Some experiences are beyond words or if you have not experienced what the writer is talking about then there will be inherent difficulties. This is particularly so when reading the work of Martin Buber.

"The fiery stuff of all my ability to will seethes tremendously, all that I might do circles around me, still without actuality in the world, flung together and seemingly inseparable, alluring glimpses of powers flicker from all the uttermost bonds; the universe is my temptation, and I achieve being in an instant, with both hands plunged deep into the fire, where the single deed is hidden, the deed which aims at me – now is the moment!"

(Buber, 1958, pg 51-52)

Third and perhaps most importantly, is the higher is descending to the lower. We are speaking at one state of being, while what we are speaking about may only be experienced at a higher or more expanded state of being. Usually the mark of this is that what is understandable at the higher or expanded state sounds paradoxical at the lower state.

Wilson Van Dusen, a psychologist, mystic and a colleague of Carl Rodgers and Fritz Perls, has the following to say on the self and the experience of the holy:

"There is another aspect of the mystical experience that seems to be consistently misunderstood. It is as if we must die to ourselves in order to see God.

This leads us to all sorts of efforts to overcome the self. This is an impossible paradox, for the one struggling against the self turns out simply to be the self. In a way the self is actually intensified by the effort to get rid of it.

The truth is that in a mystical experience there is an expansion of self – quite the opposite. It is as though God is always present and is the root and source of our very life.
God need only expand our awareness to come into consciousness."

The Country of Spirit
Wilson Van Dusen

This holds the paradox without shattering the beauty. This experience of losing self may seem at first theoretical and wordy. Words do not always convey the experience which behind the words. As we have seen this is sometimes better expressed through poetry, or art or music. This sense of losing oneself and becoming part of something bigger is not limited to such esoteric concepts. It may be found in everyday reality: in painting, in music, being in nature, cheering on your football team, being in a family gathering and laughing. There are so many areas where that which we are involved in is the direct moment and involves love and wisdom (not sure about the football team).

At such times we "forget" our "selves" and be in the moment, beyond time and worry. While in the background there is a sense of "me" - this me is almost gone, enrapt in the greater All that we are a part of. Such states are hard to translate into to words at times, and sometimes poetry achieves this best.

Gestalt, Spirituality and Community

Authors such as Polster (2006) propose community can be traced to the evolution of psychotherapy from religion. He argues that current psychotherapy as originated by

Freud and others came as a development from religion. Yet as therapy developed and borrowed from religion it left behind a most important element, that of community. He has voiced the possibility of creating communities guided by the principles of psychotherapy and the sacred as suiting the development of communities.

He states –

> *They are, I believe, on the cutting edge of psychotherapy's advance into a new paradigm, one with which religion has long been identified: the orientation and guidance of people in navigating the larger realm of everyday living.*
>
> *(Polster, E., 2008)*

As we note this paradoxical nature of self, there is alongside the individualistic perspective a primacy of social bonds in which people are reflections of an interpersonal whole. This interpersonal whole is described as a dynamic unity of need and social convention, in which men discover themselves and one another and invent themselves and one another. This conceptualisation by Perls, Hefferline and Goodman (1951) that people discover and invent each other, are involved in a co-creation, is a step towards a communal attitude. The additional element to a community, which lifts it beyond individualism into holism, is in the statement, so well explained in the book of Perls, Hefferline and Goodman, that –

The greatest value in the Gestalt approach perhaps lies in the insight that the whole determines the parts.
(Perls, et. al., 1951, pg xi)

We can enter into to these patterns of communities with the middle mode of an artist, where the community won't happen by me but it won't happen without me.

"The common celebration of the great sacrificial feasts and sacred rites, which gave expression simultaneously to the interrelation and social articulation of family and state, was the means employed by great rulers to unite men. The sacred music and splendour of the ceremonies aroused a strong tide of emotion that was shared by all hearts in unison, and that awakened a consciousness of the common origin of all creatures."

(Wilhelm, 1927/1975, pp, 227-228)

This attitude requires a paradoxical surrender yet active engagement with community process. The ground of gestalt theory has buried within it gems of principles which, further developed and explained, can foster a clarity about how to be in community as gestalt therapists, as wise children and artists in full presence to the emergence of our field of life and celebration of friends and family.

Bibliography.

Bohm, D & Hiley, B.J. (1993). The Undivided Universe. Routledge, London.

Bohr, N. (1961) Atomic Physics and Human Knowledge, Science Editions, New York.

Bowman, C. (2005). The History and Development of Gestalt Therapy in Woldt, A. and Toman, S.(2005) Gestalt Therapy: History, Theory, Practice. SAGE Publications, Thousand Oaks.

Buber, M., (1958) I-Thou, Scribner Books, New York

Capra, F. (1982) The Tao of Physics, Flamingo, London.

Crocker, S. (1999) A Well Lived Life: Essays in Gestalt Therapy. GIC Press Cleveland

Einstein, A & Infield, L. (1938) The Evolution of Physics. Simon and Schuster, New York

Ellis, W. ed.,(1938 reprinted 1997). A Source Book of Gestalt Psychology.The Gestalt Journal Press, New York

Gibran, K. (1924). *The Prophet*. NY: Alfred A. Knopf, Inc.

Hycner, R. (1995). The Healing Relationship in Gestalt Therapy: A Dialogic – Self-Psychology Approach.

Fagan, J and Shepherd, I.L. The Tasks of the Therapist in Fagan, J. and Shepherd, I.L. (1970) Gestalt Therapy Now, Science and Behavior Books, Palo Alto.

Francis, T. (2005) Working with the Field. British Gestalt Journal, 14, 1, pp 26-33.

Hamlyn, D.W. (1987) The Penguin History of Western Philosophy. Penguin Books, London.

James, W. (1902) The Varieties of Religious Experience, 1977 Fontana Paperback, Glasgow.

Kempler. W., (!974) Principles of Gestalt Family Therapy, Kempler Institute,California.

Kepner, J. (1995) Healing Tasks: Psychotherapy with Adult Survivors of Childhood Abuse. Jossey-Bass and Gestalt Institute of Cleveland, San Francisco.

Latner, J. (1983) This is the speed of light: Field and systems theory in Gestalt therapy. The Gestalt Journal,6,2 (Fall 1983), 71-90

Lee, R. (Ed) (2004) The Values of Connection: A Relational Approach to Ethics. GIC Press, Cleveland.

Le Shan, (1974) The Medium, the Mystic and the Physicist. Ballantine Books, New York

Lewin, K. (1936) Principles of Topological Psychology. McGraw-Hill, New York

Lewin, K.(1951)   Field Theory in Social Science.   University   of   Chicago   Press, Chicago.

Lightman, A (2000). Great Ideas in Physics. McGraw-Hill, New York

Mackewen, J.(1997).   Developing Gestalt Counselling, Sage Publications, London.

McNamara, W., (1979). "Mystical Passion - The Art of Christian Loving" San Francisco: Harper & Row, pages 57-58

McTaggart, L. (2003) The Field. Harper Collins, London.

Mitchell, S. (translator) (2000) The Bhagavad Bhagavad Gita. Three Rivers Press, New York.

Nicoll, M (1976) Living Time and the Integration of Life. Watkins, London.

Ornstein, R. (1972) The Psychology of Consciousness, Penguin, New York

O'Neill, B., Post Relativistic Quantum Field Theory and Gestalt Therapy, *Gestalt Review*, Vol 12, no 1, 2008, pps 7-23.

O'Neill, B., & O'Neill, J. *The Use of Group in Training*, in Feder, R., *Beyond the Hot Seat: Group Approaches in Gestalt Therapy*, Gestalt Institute Press, USA, 2008

O'Neill, B., & O'Neill, J. (2008) *Field Theory and Couples Therapy*, in Lee, R., The Secret Language of Intimacy, Routledge Press/Gestalt Press, USA,

O'Neill, B., & Gaffney, S. (2008) The Application of a Field Perspective Methodology, in Brownell, P., Handbook for Theory, Research and Practice in Gestalt Therapy, Cambridge Scholars Publishing, Cambridge.

O'Neill, B. (2010). Being Present to the Creative Emergence of the Field: Wordsworth, Buber and Gestalt Therapy. Gestalt Review, Vol 14, 2.

O'Neill, B. (2012) *Gestalt Family Therapy* in Levine Bar-Yoseph, T., (ed) New Approaches to Gestalt Therapy, Routledge, London.

O'Neill, B. (2012) A Quantum of Gestalt: Physics, Spirituality and Gestalt Therapy. Ravenwood Press, Australia.

Parlett, M.(1993). Towards a More Lewian Gestalt Therapy, British Gestalt Journal, 2,2 p. 115-121

Parlett, M.(1997). The Unified Field in Practice. Gestalt Review, 1,1 p.16-33

Parlett, M. (2005) Contemporary Gestalt Therapy: Field Theory in Woldt, A. & Toman, S. Gestalt Therapy: History, Theory and Practice. Sage Publications, Thousand Oaks.

Perls, F., Hefferline, R., and Goodman, P. (1951) Gestalt Therapy: Excitement and Growth in the Human Personality. Souvenir Press edition (1984) London.

Philippson. P. (2002) Self in Relation. Gestalt Journal Press, New York.

Polster, E. & Polster, M. (1973) Gestalt therapy integrated: Contours of theory and practice. Brunner-Mazel, New York.

Polster, E & Polster, M. (1999) From the Radical Center: The Heart of Gestalt Therapy. GIC Press, Cleveland.

Resnick, R. (1995). Gestalt therapy: Principles, prisms and perspectives. British Gestalt Journal,4(1),3-13.

Robine, J.(2001) From Field to Situation in Robine, J (Ed) Contact and Relationship in a Field Perspective. L'experimerie Bordeaux.

Sheldrake, R.(2003) The Sense of Being Stared At and other aspects of the Extended Mind. Random House, London.
Shepard, M (1976) Fritz. Bantam, New York

Smuts, J. (1926) edited by Holst, S. (1999) Holism and Evolution: The Original Source of the Holistic Approach to Life. Sierra Sunrise Books.

Staemmler, F.M.(2006). A Babylonian Confusion? – The Term Field. The British Gestalt Journal, 15:2 : 64-83

Swedenborg, E. (1768, edition 1992) Conjugial Love, Swedenborg Foundation, New York

Swedenborg, E. (1758, edition 2009) Heaven and Its Wonders and Hell, Swedenborg Foundation, New York pg 31-32

Talbot, M.(1991) The Holographic Universe. Harper Collins, London.

Tart, C., (1975) States of Consciousness. E P Dutton and Co, New York.

Van Dusen, W. (1975) Invoking the Actual, in Stevens, J.O., gestalt is, Real People Press, Moab.

Wheeler, G (1991) Gestalt Reconsidered: A New Approach to Contact and Resistance. GIC Press, Cleveland.

Wheeler, G. (2000). *Beyond Individualism: Towards a New Understanding of Self, Relationship and Experience.* Hillsdale, NJ: Gestalt Institute of Cleveland Press.

Van Dusen, W. (2001). *The Design of Existence.* Chrysalis Books, West Chester,

Wertheimer, M. Gestalt Theory. (1925) in
Ellis, W. ed.,(1938 reprinted 1997). A
Source Book of Gestalt Psychology.The
Gestalt Journal Press, New York

Wilber, K. (ed) (1985) The Holographic
Paradigm and Other Paradoxes.
Shambhala, Boston & London.

Yontef, G. (1993) Awareness, Dialogue and
Process: Essays of Gestalt Therapy. The
Gestalt Journal Press, New York,

Zinker, J. (1994) In search of good form:
Gestalt therapy with couples and families.
Jossey- Bass, San Francisco.